e-Citizen™

Published by:

CiA Training Ltd
Business & Innovation Centre
Sunderland Enterprise Park
Sunderland SR5 2TH
United Kingdom

Tel: +44 (0) 191 549 5002
Fax: +44 (0) 191 549 9005

info@ciatraining.co.uk
www.ciatraining.co.uk

ISBN 1-86005-238-X

Release EC001v1

First published 2004

Copyright © 2004 CiA Training Ltd

Microsoft is a registered trademark and Windows is a trademark of the Microsoft Corporation. Screen images reproduced by permission of the Microsoft Corporation. All other trademarks in this book are acknowledged as the property of their respective owners.

Inland Revenue screen grabs reproduced by permission of © Crown copyright 2002. Additional screen grabs reproduced by permission of Google Incorporated and Fish4.

European Computer Driving Licence, ECDL and logo, ECDL, International Computer Driving Licence, ICDL and logo, ICDL, and e-Citizen are trade marks of The European Computer Driving Licence Foundation Limited ("ECDL-F") in Ireland and other countries.

CiA Training Ltd is an entity independent of ECDL-F and is not associated with ECDL-F in any manner. This courseware publication may be used to assist candidates to prepare for the e-Citizen test. Neither ECDL-F nor CiA Training Ltd warrants that the use of this courseware publication will ensure passing of the e-Citizen test. Use of the ECDL-F Approved Courseware logo on this courseware publication signifies that it has been independently reviewed and approved by ECDL-F as complying with the following standard:

Technical compliance with the learning objectives of e-Citizen Syllabus Version 1.0

The material contained in this courseware publication has not been reviewed for technical accuracy and does not guarantee that candidates will pass the e-Citizen test. Any and all assessment items and/or performance-based exercises contained in this courseware publication relate solely to this publication and do not constitute or imply certification by ECDL-F in respect of the e-Citizen test or any other ECDL-F test.

For details on sitting the e-Citizen test and other ECDL-F tests in your country, please contact your country's National ECDL/ICDL designated Licensee or visit ECDL-F's web site at www.ecdl.com.

Candidates using this courseware publication must register before undertaking the e-Citizen test. Without a valid registration, the e-Citizen test cannot be undertaken and no e-Citizen certificate, nor any other form of recognition, can be given to a candidate. You may register at any Approved e-Citizen Test Centre.

e-Citizen Syllabus Version 1.0 is the official syllabus of the e-Citizen certification programme at the date of approval of this courseware publication.

The exercises/information contained within this manual and on the websites/CD are not e-Citizen tests. To locate your nearest e-Citizen test centre please go to the ECDL Foundation website at www.ecdl.com.

CiA Training's guide for *e-Citizen™* is a collection of structured exercises to provide support for each block of the new qualification. The exercises build into a complete open learning package covering the entire syllabus, to equip the user to confidently carry out a wide variety of online tasks and access various types of information.

This guide was created using *Windows XP* but is referenced for use with *Windows 2000*; screen grabs shown are from *Windows XP*. If earlier versions of Windows are used, there may be subtle differences. It assumes that a printer and mouse are attached to the computer.

e-Citizen - The guide supporting this core unit contains exercises covering the following topics:

- Main Parts of a Computer
- Starting & Shutting Down the Computer
- Using the Mouse
- Using the Taskbar and Menus
- Working with Windows
- Using Simple Applications
- Saving Work

- Understanding File Management
- Understanding Internet Basics
- Understanding E-mail Basics
- Searching For and Saving Information
- Awareness of Security Issues
- Accessing Online Services
- Using Online Services

Aims and Objectives

To provide the knowledge and techniques necessary for the attainment of a certificate in this qualification. After completing the guide the user will be able to:

- Operate a computer, understand hardware and software, handle files and folders, work with windows, use simple applications, browse the Internet and use e-mail.
- Use search techniques to browse for information, be aware of the risks associated with Internet use.
- Confidently carry out everyday tasks online, but appreciate the security measures necessary to do this.

This guide is suitable for:

- Any individual wishing to obtain the e-Citizen qualification. No prior knowledge of *Windows* is required. The user works through the guide from start to finish.

- Tutor led groups as reinforcement material. It can be used as and when necessary.

Introduction

This guide assumes that *Windows* has been correctly and <u>fully</u> installed on your personal computer. Some features described in this guide may not work if the program was not **fully** installed. It is assumed that the default settings are in operation. *Windows* has a hierarchical system of users. Each user is given a particular status that governs what they can and cannot do. The types of user are: **Administrators**, **Power Users**, **Restricted Users**.

Notation Used Throughout This Guide

- Key presses are included within < > e.g. **<Enter>** means press the **Enter** key.

- Menu selections are written, e.g. **File | Open** means select the **File** menu and then from the list of commands that appears, select **Open**.

- Where the operation of *Windows 2000* differs from *Windows XP*, extra information is provided and is indicated by the ▦ symbol. General help and tips are indicated by the ◈ symbol.

- The guide is split into individual exercises. Each exercise consists of a written explanation of the feature, followed by a stepped exercise. Read the notes carefully and then follow the steps, with reference to the notes if necessary.

Recommendations

- Work through the exercises in sequence, so that one feature is understood before moving on to the next.

- Read the whole of each exercise before starting to work through it. This ensures the understanding of the topic and prevents unnecessary mistakes.

Important Notes For All Users

Much of the guide can be worked through using our supplied simulated web sites, without the need to connect to real sites on the Internet. This is to build confidence in the features before tackling them live. Where interaction with live Internet sites is required, instructions will be shown in a shaded box. The simulated web sites have been specially created to use with this guide. They are available at the following address: *www.learnersworld.co.uk.* Alternatively, some organisations may prefer to work with these sites offline; they can be obtained on CD for an additional cost. Contact our sales team at the address on page 2.

This book contains instructions to visit other web sites of interest. However, once you have left the simulated sites you should note that CiA does not have any control over any other web site. Therefore, CiA cannot be responsible for the protection and privacy of any information which you provide whilst visiting such sites. You should exercise caution and look at the privacy statement applicable to the web site in question.

Web sites are constantly changing. At the time of writing, all addresses and links are correct, but this <u>may</u> change. If a named web site is unavailable, you will need to search for an alternative. A list of useful web sites is provided at the back of this guide.

For product related support, visit ***www.ciasupport.co.uk*** *or e-mail contact@ciasupport.co.uk.*

e-Citizen
© CiA Training Ltd 2004

Block 1

Foundation Skills

This Block gives you the necessary skills and knowledge for basic computer and Internet use. You will learn about computer hardware and software, be able to handle files and folders and know how to work with icons and windows on a computer screen.

You will also be able to create a simple document, browse the Internet and use e-mail.

© CiA Training Ltd 2004

CD-R. - can add to it
CD-RW - Change INFO add + delete.

Chapter 1 - The Computer

In this chapter you will learn how to: recognise the main parts of a computer, switch the computer on, recognise the *Windows* **Desktop**, use the mouse, **Taskbar** and **Start** menu, manipulate windows, shut down the computer properly.

Introduction to the Computer

A computer can be terrifying; it's a fact - especially when you don't even know how to switch it on (this can be a problem for experienced users, the on/off switch can often be well disguised). However, once you get to know them, computers can be fun to use and can make your life much easier. Computers are also more robust than you might think; in normal operation it is almost impossible to break them and is actually quite easy to correct any mistakes you may make!

This exercise will help you to become familiar with the different parts of a computer. Even though the appearance of each of the computer system components can vary greatly, the basic configuration of the system will be the same.

CD-ROM Drive

Floppy Disk Drive

Case contains Processing Unit

On/Off Switch

Monitor

Mouse

Keyboard

This shows a "tower" type of computer system

e-Citizen
© CiA Training Ltd 2004

Exercise 1

1. Use the previous diagram to identify the **keyboard**. This is an **Input Device**, used to type (input) information into the computer.

2. Now find the **monitor** or Visual Display Unit (**VDU**), an **Output Device**. This is used to view information entered into the computer. It looks like a television screen.

3. Locate the **mouse**, which gets its name from the "tail" (wire) that attaches it to the computer. When you move the mouse around on its **mouse mat**, a cursor, moves in the same direction on the monitor. The mouse enables you to select options shown on the screen. Later exercises will teach you how to do this.

4. The computer case, a big plastic box, found either underneath the monitor, or at one side (depending on the type of computer you have) contains the "brains" - the **central processing unit** (**CPU**) motherboard, microchips, etc. - and wiring which allow the whole thing to work. This is the most important part of the system.

5. The **hard disk drive** (**HDD**), the main storage device which is used to store programs and data, is found inside this box.

6. Find the **floppy disk drive** (**FDD**). It may lie horizontally, or turned sideways, but will have a little button (used to eject disks) next to it. This drive allows you to insert a floppy disk (shown here), so that you can transfer work to and from the computer.

7. Most computers also have a **CD-ROM drive** to read information from a compact disk (CD), which can contain software, information or music. Try to find this drive on your computer.

    To insert a CD, press the **Eject** button, ⏏, to open the drive. Place the CD, label side up into the "drawer" and press the same button to close the drive.

8. Your computer may have **speakers** attached, to play music or listen to communications. Can you find any speakers? They may be part of the computer rather than separate from it.

9. Make sure you know where all these parts are on your computer. They are known as **hardware**. Computer **software** consists of the programs that allow you to use the computer, such as the operating system (*Windows*), games, word processor or spreadsheet applications. You can touch hardware but not software.

Starting the Computer

The processing unit has to be switched on to load the operating system, which enables the computer to work. This is done using the **Power** or **On/Off** button.

Exercise 2

1. Before switching a computer on, check that there are no lights, usually green, on the front of the computer, which shows that the computer is already powered.

2. If there is a light on, but no display, the computer is probably in a dormant state. Move the mouse or press a key on the keyboard to reactivate it. If there is still no display, the monitor may be switched off. If there is no light on the monitor, switch it on. Read the remaining steps of this exercise for reference.

3. If the computer is not on, check the floppy drive for disks. If there is a disk in the drive, remove it by pressing the small button next to the drive.

4. Press the **Power Switch** on the front of the computer. If no lights come on, check all leads are firmly in place.

5. If the monitor power light does not come on, press the monitor power button (some monitors take their power from the computer, some have their own power lead).

6. When both units are powered, wait while the computer goes through a start-up routine and displays information on the screen.

7. After various checks the *Windows* operating system is loaded.

8. If the computer you are working on is networked (joined to other computers), a **Network Password** dialog box may appear, prompting for a password. This is known as **logging on**. Enter your **User name** and **Password**. Use the keyboard to type these in.

9. When the information has been entered in the boxes, either move the mouse until the arrow is over **OK** and then use the left mouse button to click on **OK**, or press the <**Enter**> key on the keyboard.

    You may need some help logging on, if you have never used the keyboard or mouse before. The next exercises will help you, but ask someone to show you what to do to at this stage.

10. The *Windows* **Desktop** screen is displayed.

The Windows Desktop

The *Windows* operating system uses a **Graphical User Interface** (**GUI**), which is a way of showing the computer's facilities using **icons** (pictures), **menus** (lists of names), and **buttons**. Instead of typing a technical instruction, the mouse is used to click on an icon, menu or button to select or perform an action. Icons can be seen on the **Desktop**.

The way the **Desktop** looks can be changed to suit the computer user. Icons can be added for a variety of functions, some Desktops may be almost filled with icons. The size and shape of icons can vary, and a vast range of background colours, pictures and effects is available. For these reasons, *the screens shown in this guide may look quite different to those of your computer*. Don't worry, because the basic operation should be the same.

Exercise 3

1. The screen shows the **Desktop**. This is the work area for all tasks performed in *Windows*. From here it is possible to access all the programs on the computer, manage how it works and use all the features of *Windows*.

2. The screen is similar to the one shown below. Your screen may have more or different icons and patterns or a picture as a background rather than a plain colour.

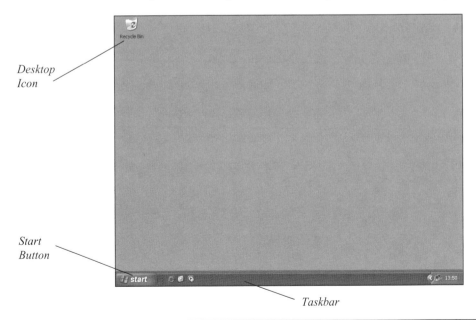

Desktop Icon

Start Button

Taskbar

3. The **Desktop** is divided into two parts. Along the bottom of the screen is a bar known as the **Taskbar**. This is used as a quick way to access certain features and usually remains on screen at all times. **Icons** (small pictures with text, e.g. the **Recycle Bin**, and **Internet Explorer**, , icons) take up the remainder of the **Desktop**.

4. These icons represent programs saved on the **Desktop** or shortcuts that lead directly to a program, folder, file, etc. They will be used later.

The Keyboard

You will need to use both the keyboard (see example below) and the mouse to enter information into the computer.

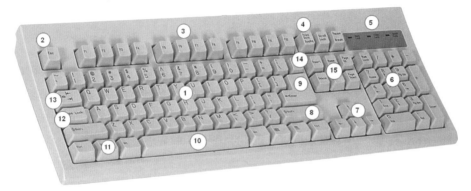

The computer keyboard contains the following features:

1	**Typewriter keyboard**	used to type in text, symbols and numbers
2	**Esc**	the escape key, an alternative to a **Cancel** option
3	**Function keys F1 - F12**	used to access shortcuts in some programs
4	**Print Screen**	copies the exact content shown on screen, so it can then be printed
5	**Indicator lights**	show if any locks are activated, such as **Caps Lock**
6	**Numeric keypad**	also includes mathematical keys, **+**, **-**, etc. Numbers can be entered more quickly using these keys. The number lock must be on to use this keypad - use the top left button on the keypad (**Num Lock**) to switch it on or off

handwritten annotations: ✗ Open Word – Paste – Print   Can be used   ✗ multiply – Divide   to use Numeric Keypad go to Accessories and bring up prog. and a calculator

e-Citizen
© CiA Training Ltd 2004

7	Arrow keys	allow movement around a text document, for example
8	Shift	hold this down to type a capital letter, or a symbol above another, e.g. £ above the 3
9	Enter	used to enter information, or to start a new line when typing
10	Spacebar	adds one space to text
11	Ctrl, Alt	used in combination with other keys to perform various functions
12	Caps Lock	types in capitals until pressed again
13	Tab	moves along the page to the next tab stop, set at regular intervals to help line up text
14	Backspace	used to delete text to the left of the cursor
15	Delete/directional keys	**Delete** is used to delete text to the right of the cursor. The directional keys, e.g. **Home**, **Page Up** allow a greater degree of movement around a document

The Mouse

Nearly all *Windows* tasks can be performed using the mouse. There are a few different mouse techniques, they are:

Point	position the mouse pointer until the tip of the pointer on the screen rests on the required position
Click	press and immediately release the left mouse button without moving the mouse
Double click	click the left mouse button twice in rapid succession
Right click	click with the right button of the mouse
Click and Drag	press the mouse button and hold it down while the mouse is moved, then release the button at the appropriate location

Both the left and right mouse buttons are used to perform different tasks in Windows. Unless stated, use the left mouse button. If your mouse has three buttons, ignore the one in the centre.

Exercise 4

1. With the mouse in the centre of a suitable mouse mat, rest your hand over the mouse with the fingers positioned over the buttons as shown here.

2. Lightly grip the mouse and slowly move it around on the mat. The mouse pointer, ⇖, on the screen should mirror the movements you make with your hand.

3. If your **Desktop** has icons for **My Computer**, **My Documents** and **Recycle Bin** proceed to step 9.

4. To add the **My Computer** icon to the **Desktop** click once on **start** at the bottom left of the screen.

> **Ian Chapman**
>
> Paint Shop Pro 4
> Microsoft Project
> Microsoft Access
> Microsoft Word
> Microsoft Excel
> Microsoft FrontPage
> Internet Explorer
> Microsoft PowerPoint
>
> My Documents
> My Recent Documents ▸
> My Pictures
> My Music
> My Computer
> My Network Places
> Control Panel
> Connect To ▸
> Printers and Faxes
> Help and Support
> Search
> Run...
>
> All Programs ▷
>
> Log Off   Turn Off Computer

5. Point at **My Computer** and click the <u>right</u> mouse button to display a menu.

6. Click on the **Show on Desktop** option.

7. Click on a blank part of the **Desktop** to close the menu and see the new **My Computer** icon.

8. Repeat steps 4 to 7 to create an icon for **My Documents** and again for **Recycle Bin**.

9. Move the mouse pointer over the **My Computer** icon on the screen. Holding the mouse steady, click once on the icon. It becomes highlighted (darker) to show that it has been **selected**.

10. Move the mouse to a clear part of the **Desktop** and click to **deselect** the icon.

    *Usually in **Windows**, one click selects an item and double clicking performs an operation, such as opening a folder or running a program.*

11. Move the mouse over the **My Computer** icon again, hold it steady and quickly click twice. If you have managed to double click correctly you should now be able to see a new area called a **window** open on top of the **Desktop**. This is the **My Computer** window.

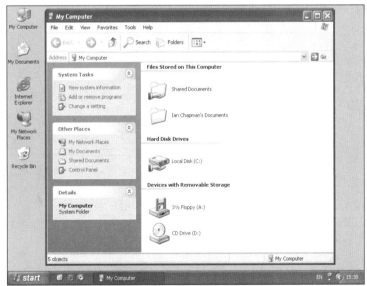

Your window may look different to the diagram

12. If the window is not visible, just click once on a blank part of the screen, then try again to double click on the **My Computer** icon. You will need to click quickly.

    Information within a window can be displayed in a variety of ways. Do not worry if your window does not match the one above.

13. If the window fills the screen click once on the **Restore Down** button, , at the top right of the screen.

14. Windows are dealt with a little later, but for now, the **My Computer** window needs to be closed. At the top right corner of the window there is a button with a cross, . Move the mouse pointer over the cross and notice the **Screen Tip**, **Close**. Click once on the cross to close the window.

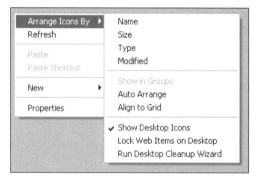

15. Now try right clicking. Move the mouse pointer over a blank part of the **Desktop** and click once with the right mouse button. A **Shortcut Menu** is displayed. A menu is a list of options from which a selection can be made.

16. Place the cursor over **Arrange Icons By** (in *Windows 2000 Arrange Icons*) and a further menu appears.

17. If **Auto Arrange** has a tick on the left (to show this option is currently selected), then click on the word **Auto Arrange** to turn it off ready for the next operation when you will learn how to click and drag.

> ⓘ *Auto Arrange* keeps the icons in place on the left, so they cannot be moved.

18. If the menus are still on screen, click once on a blank area of the screen to remove them.

19. Click on any icon, hold the left mouse button down and drag the icon around the screen by moving the mouse.

20. Release the mouse button to place the icon at the new position.

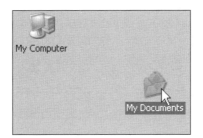

21. Move the icon back to its original position.

22. By clicking and dragging, move some of the icons around the **Desktop**.

23. Right click on a blank part of the screen to display the shortcut menu, point to **Arrange Icons By** and click with the left button on **Align to Grid** (🖽 *in Windows 2000 this is called Line Up Icons*) if it is not already checked. This means the icons are kept in the same order but automatically spaced.

24. Click with the right mouse button again, select the **Arrange Icons By** option and then **Name**. The icons on the **Desktop** are now arranged neatly, in alphabetical order by name.

    ⓘ *The icons may already have been arranged by name, so no sorting may be seen.*

25. Click with the right mouse button again and select **Arrange Icons By | Size**. The icons are now arranged with the largest file first.

26. Rearrange the icons by **Name** again.

27. Reapply the **Auto Arrange** option if required.

    ⓘ *The arranging of icons on the **Desktop** has more impact for those screens containing a large number of icons.*

The Start Menu

The **Start** menu is a useful feature within *Windows*, as seen already. This is displayed by clicking the **Start** button at the left of the **Taskbar**. Although there may be icons on the **Desktop**, used to start many of the more commonly used programs, the **Start** menu can be used to find and start any program that has been installed on the computer.

Like the **Desktop**, the appearance of the **Start** menu can be varied by the user. In addition *Windows* itself continuously changes the content of the menu by ensuring that recently used applications are always included.

> ⊞ *In **Windows 2000** the menu content does not change with application use.*

Exercise 5

1. Click the **Start** button to display the **Start** menu. For the reasons stated above, the contents and appearance of this menu may be different to that shown here.

2. Place the mouse pointer over **All Programs** (⊞ *in **Windows 2000** this is Programs*) to display the list of programs installed (it will probably be different to that shown below).

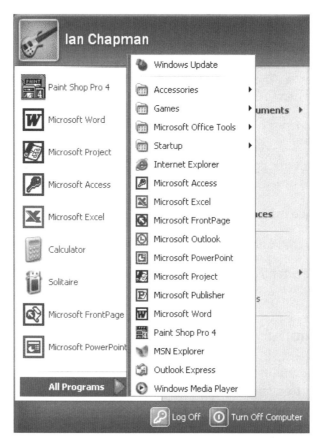

3. Move the mouse pointer over the **Games** to display that menu group.

 *In **Windows 2000 Games** is stored within **Accessories**.*

FreeCell

Hearts

Internet Backgammon

Internet Checkers

Internet Hearts

Internet Reversi

Internet Spades

Minesweeper

Pinball

Solitaire

Spider Solitaire

Windows 2000 has fewer games.

4. Now click **Solitaire** and you can play a game of cards.

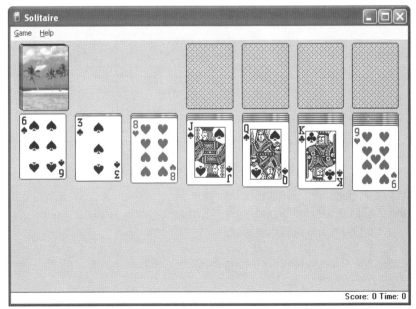

5. This game will allow you to perfect your click and drag technique. The cards are moved by clicking and dragging from one pile to another and turned over by clicking once. They can be placed on one of the four blank areas at the top right by either double clicking or dragging.

    > *If you don't know how to play **Solitaire**, click on the **Help** menu at the top of the game window then click **Search for Help on**. Click on the **Index** tab and double click **how to play**. Read the help at the right. Click **Close**, [X], at the top right of the window to close help.*

6. To close **Solitaire**, click on the **Game** menu at the top of the **Solitaire** window and then click **Exit**.

7. To start another application, click **start** then **All Programs**, then **Accessories** and finally **Calculator**. The **Calculator** window is displayed.

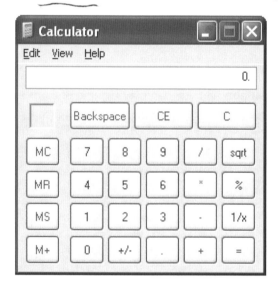

8. Use the calculator by either typing the required calculation on the numeric keypad at the right of the keyboard (use **<Enter>** as the answer button), or selecting the required numbers and operators using the mouse.

9. Close the **Calculator** by clicking its **Close** button, [X].

Windows

Windows gets its name from the fact that everything you do on the computer is shown in a window. Think of working with the computer as looking through a window to see the information stored inside the computer.

Windows come in various sizes, but are always rectangular and have several features in common. Many windows can be open at the same time although you can only interact with one at a time (the active window). Windows can be manipulated separately and are often placed on top of one another. The **Taskbar** will show you the windows that are open. Look at the diagram below:

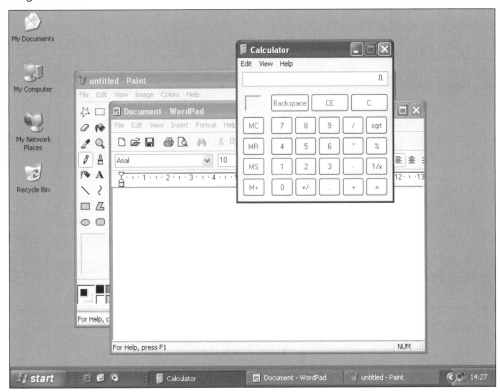

The diagram above shows Windows XP with three application windows open

There are three windows open on the **Desktop**, one on top of another. The **Calculator** window is active. The following exercises will show you how to work with windows, although you have already encountered some by working through earlier exercises.

Exercise 6

1. Move the mouse pointer until it is over the **My Computer** icon on the **Desktop**. Double click the left mouse button.

2. The **My Computer** window will open (some icons may be different to those shown below).

*The above diagram shows a window in **Classic View**, displaying **Icons**.*

3. If your window has an extra panel at the left, click the **Tools** menu and select **Folder Options**.

4. With the **General** tab displayed, click the **Use Windows classic folders** option and click **OK** to apply the classic folders settings.

5. The contents of windows that show folders or files can be viewed in a variety of ways. The view of each window can be set independently. Select the **View** menu and then the **Icons** option.

6. The application name is displayed on the **Title Bar** of the open window and a button, ![My Computer], appears on the **Taskbar**. Each separate, opened window is represented by a button on the **Taskbar**.

7. Each window is similar in its construction. A **Title Bar** is across the top normally coloured blue. At the top right of the **Title Bar** are three **Window Control Buttons**. These are the **Minimize,** [■] **, Maximize,** [□] and **Close,** [X], buttons.

    *If the window fills the screen the centre button will be **Restore Down,** [▣] ; click this button to reduce the size of the window.*

8. Below the **Title Bar** is the **Menu Bar** - each name leads to a drop down menu. Click **File** and view the list. Move the mouse over each menu name in turn to view its list.

9. Notice that some of the items are ghosted, greyed out; this means that they are not currently available.

10. Click on the menu name again or click on any blank part of the window to close the menu.

11. Below the **Menu Bar** is the **Toolbar**. This is a row of buttons to quickly achieve tasks without using the alternative menu option.

12. Within the window point to and click the **Hard Disk Drive** icon, Local Disk (C:).

    It changes to Local Disk (C:) when selected.

    *The **Hard Disk Drive** is where all the information is stored on a computer. It is nearly always known as the **C** drive, written as **(C:)**. If the drive is shared with other networked computers, the icon will look like the one in the diagram on page 28.*

13. From the menu, select **File** and then **Properties**. This opens a **Dialog Box** (it cannot be resized) displaying the amount of used and free space on the hard disk drive.

14. Click **Cancel** to close this dialog box.

15. The **Close** button, [X], at the top right of every window, closes it and also any task that may be running within it. Locate the **Close** button on the **My Computer** window and click on it. IT CAN ALSO BE DONE Y <ALT> + 1ST <F4> 2ND

    *A window can also be closed by holding down the <**Alt**> key on the keyboard and pressing the <**F4**> key, then releasing <**Alt**>.*

Block 1 Foundation Skills

Manipulating Windows

Windows can be made to fill the screen (**maximised**), or to be hidden completely (**minimised**). **Restoring** a window changes a maximised window back to its previous intermediate size. When a window is in this state, its size and position can be adjusted. These actions can be collectively called manipulating windows.

Exercise 7

1. Open **My Computer** by double clicking on its icon.

2. If the window is not already maximised, click the **Maximize** button, 🔲, on the **My Computer** window so that it fills the screen.

3. When a window is maximised, the **Maximize** button is replaced by the **Restore Down** button, 🗗. Click the **Restore Down** button to change the maximised window back to its previous size.

4. Move the mouse pointer over the **Title Bar** of the **My Computer** window.

5. Click and drag downwards. The entire window will move down. Be careful, it is possible to move part of the window off the screen.

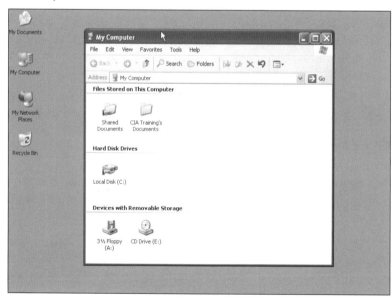

e-Citizen
© CiA Training Ltd 2004

ONLY (handwritten)

6. The size of the window can also be changed. Move the mouse pointer over the right edge of the window, until the pointer changes to a black double headed arrow, ↔.

7. Click and drag to the right, and then release the mouse button, to increase the width of the window.

8. Placing the mouse over a corner of a window allows a two-directional change in the size of a window. Place the mouse pointer over the bottom right corner of the **My Computer** window. *O NLY THE* (handwritten)

9. The cursor changes to a two headed diagonal arrow, ⬉. Click and drag a small amount in any direction to change the size and scale of the window.

10. The **Minimize** button, ▬, hides the window completely. Click the **Minimize** button on the **My Computer** window.

11. The window disappears but it is not closed. Any tasks running in this window will still be running. The window can be re-activated at any time by clicking on its button on the **Taskbar**, at the bottom of the screen. Click the **My Computer** button, 🖳 My Computer, on the **Taskbar**. The window appears again.

12. Double click 📁 My Documents (move or resize the **My Computer** window first if necessary to see the **Desktop** icons) and if the window is maximised, click the **Restore Down** button.

13. Double click 🗑 Recycle Bin on the **Desktop**. There are now three open windows and three buttons on the **Taskbar**.

> 🛈 *When there are too many open windows to fit in the **Taskbar** an alternative display is sometimes used. Clicking the arrow at the right of the button will reveal the names of the individual windows in the group.*

CWHG16 (handwritten)

📁 3 Windows Explorer ▾

14. If necessary, resize the windows so that they can all be seen (remember to select a window by clicking on it before trying to resize it).

SELECT SOMETHING I CLICK (handwritten)

TO OPEN = 2 CLICKS (handwritten)

95.44 (handwritten)

TITLE - TOP
TASK BAR - BOTTOM

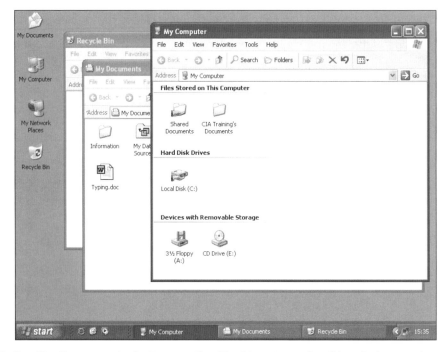

15. Click the **My Documents** button on the **Taskbar** to make this window active and bring it to the front.

16. Use any method to close all three windows.

Scroll Bars

When any window is too small to display all the information available, the window automatically adds **Scroll Bars**. Scroll Bars are added horizontally and/or vertically, depending on the hidden information.

Exercise 8

1. Select **Start | Control Panel** to open the **Control Panel** window.

   *In **Windows 2000** select **Start | Settings | Control Panel**.*

2. There are many more icons inside this window. If the window fills the screen, click **Restore Down**, , to make the **Control Panel** smaller.

3. Reduce the size of the **Control Panel** by clicking and dragging the bottom right corner of the window, until a vertical **Scroll Bar** is displayed.

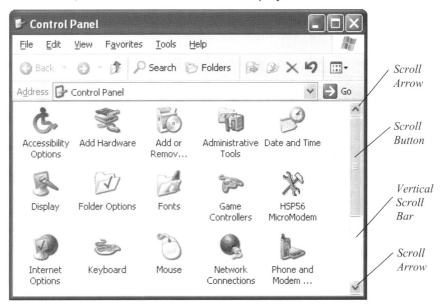

*The window above shows **Classic View***

4. A scroll bar indicates that not all of the available content for this window is being displayed. It consists of scroll arrows, top and bottom, a scroll button and an empty bar to drag the button into. The scroll bar represents the total extent of the window and the scroll button represents the proportion of the content currently displayed. In the picture above for example, the scroll bar indicates that the upper half (approximately) of the available content is shown.

> *A small button therefore indicates that there is a lot more of the window to see, and a large button indicates that most of the content is visible.*

5. Click on the down arrow of the vertical scroll bar to move the window down. Continue to do this until the scroll button is at the bottom of the scroll bar.

6. Click and drag the vertical scroll button to the top of the bar to redisplay the top part of the content.

7. Click once on the vertical scroll bar between the scroll button and the bottom arrow to move the display of a window down by exactly one screen.

BLACK. CAT. ANTIQUES
JADIE 246
JLEB 90

Scroll Arrow   Scroll Button   Scroll Bar

(i) *Some windows will have both sets of scroll bars in use at the same time.*

8.   Leave the **Control Panel** window open.

Dialog Boxes

The usual way of changing any settings or choosing options in a *Windows* application is by using dialog boxes. A dialog box is a small window that contains various options, choices and commands. There are many different ways of choosing options in a dialog box, such as buttons which are clicked, boxes which have ticks or crosses inserted in them, buttons which make lists of options appear, etc. Some of these different ways of choosing options are:

Tabs

These are small tabs at the top of the dialog box which, when clicked on, change the contents of the dialog box to a different set of choices.

Buttons	Pointers	Pointer Options	Hardware

List Boxes

A list box contains a list of options, any one of which can be chosen by clicking on it. If the list is very long, there will be a scroll bar at the right. The scroll bar has arrows at the top and bottom to move up and down.

TO GET TO TABS
GO TO DIALOG BOX
GO TO ICONS

e-Citizen
© CiA Training Ltd 2004

THEN DOUBLE CLICK ON
DISPLAY

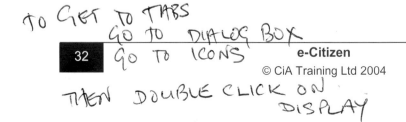

Option Buttons

Two or more option buttons may be displayed and a choice made from the alternatives. Only one option can be chosen at a time. The selected option has a small black circle in the white button.

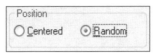

Check Boxes

These show options which can be turned on or off. To change the status of a check box, click on it. A ✔ (tick) appears in the box if the option is selected. Any number of check boxes can be selected at any time.

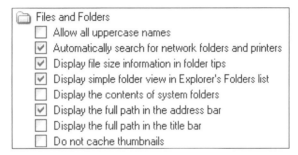

Drop Down Lists

To make a selection, click on the arrow button at the right of the box and a list of options appears. Scroll down the list to find the required option and click on it. The list disappears and the selection appears in the box.

Number Selection

When a number is required, it can be either typed into the box or the up and down spinners can be used to increase or decrease the number shown.

Spinner

Text Boxes

Text is entered in this box.

Slider Controls

Sliders are used to select a setting from an available range. Use the mouse to click and drag the slider until it is over the required setting.

Exercise 9

1. The **Control Panel** should still be open. This contains many tools used for configuring and changing the way *Windows* looks and acts.

2. In the **Control Panel** window, open the **Display** icon, Display , by double clicking on it. You may have to scroll to see this icon.

3. The **Display Properties** dialog box now appears. Use the tabs at the top of the dialog box to see all the different types of controls. Do not change any settings.

4. Click the **Cancel** button to close the dialog box so that no changes are made.

5. Close the **Control Panel** window.

Shut Down and Restart the Computer

If a computer is shut down abnormally, e.g. switched off in mid task, any unsaved data in an application can be lost and storage space within the computer can be corrupted. Shutting down properly prevents this and ensures that programs are closed and all data is saved correctly.

Normally, you should never need to restart the computer, while it's switched on. It can, however, be restarted because of problems, without switching off the power. Sometimes a computer locks up, which means that it does not respond to moving the mouse or any key presses. The only course of action in this circumstance is to restart the computer.

Exercise 10

1. To close *Windows*, make sure all applications are closed down, then click the **Start** button and select **Turn Off Computer**.

2. Click **Turn Off** (**Cancel** can be selected to return to the **Desktop**).

   *In **Windows 2000**, select **Shut Down** from the **Start** menu, select the **Shut down** option from the drop down list and then click **OK** to turn off the computer, or click **Cancel** to return to the **Desktop**.*

3. When the message appears informing you to switch off, do so (some computers switch themselves off). If the monitor light remains on, switch the monitor off as well. The computer is now switched off completely.

   *Follow these actions every time you wish to turn off the computer. Never switch the power off when the **Desktop** is displayed. ALWAYS close down Windows properly, using the **Start Menu**.*

4. Turn the computer and monitor on and wait until *Windows* is running, logging on if required.

5.   Click on **Start**, then on **Turn Off Computer** to display the **Turn off computer** box.

6.   Select **Restart** and click **OK**. The computer will restart.

> *In an emergency, if the keyboard and mouse are not responding, the **Reset** button on the front of the computer can be used to restart it.*

Exercise 11 - Revision: The Computer

1.   Which part of the computer is used to type information?
     a)   Mouse
     b)   Keyboard
     c)   Monitor
     d)   Scanner

2.   What is the term for all the physical parts of a computer, e.g. monitor, mouse, processing unit, etc?
     a)   Applications
     b)   Software
     c)   Bits
     d)   Hardware

3.   What term is used to describe the programs that allow you to use the computer?
     a)   Hardware
     b)   Desktop
     c)   Software
     d)   Microsoft Office

4.   What appears on the **Taskbar** when a window is open?
     a)   A named button representing the window
     b)   The time
     c)   The **Start** button
     d)   A **Close** button

> *The answers are listed in the **Answers Section** at the end of the guide.*

Chapter 2 - Simple Applications

In this chapter you will learn how to: run an application, enter and format text in a word processing application, save documents, print documents, close an application.

Running an Application

When an application (program) is installed on the computer, it normally adds itself somewhere into the **Start** button menus. It may add a new item under **All Programs**, or be included in an existing group of items.

Microsoft Word is one of the most frequently used applications for word processing. It allows you to create or open documents, enter or amend text using the keyboard, and print or save the results.

> (i) *If Word is not available, Windows comes with a simple word processor called* ***WordPad****, found within* ***Accessories****, which will perform most of the actions required by the following exercises.*

Exercise 12

1. Click once on [⊞ **start**] to show the list of options available.

2. Move to [**All Programs** ▶].

   ⊞ *Programs in* ***Windows 2000****.*

3. Click the application name, [**W** Microsoft Word].

   > (i) *There may be slight differences depending on individual installations. The application may have a slightly different name, or be included in a group, such as* ***Microsoft Office****. If this is the case, select the group name before the application name.*

4. Maximise the window if it does not fill the screen.

MILLAR.A.J@BLUEYONDER.CO.UK

LIANE.MILLAR@HOTMAIL.COM

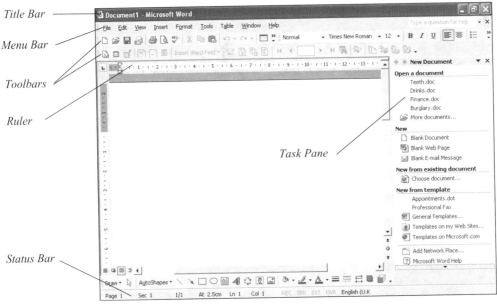

Labels (left side): Title Bar, Menu Bar, Toolbars, Ruler, Status Bar

The screen layout is typical of many Windows applications.

5. The **Task Pane** is displayed at the right of the screen by default. It changes depending on the current task and contains helpful links and shortcuts, as well as buttons to help you perform the particular task.

   Task Panes are not available in **Office 2000** *and earlier.*

6. The **Title Bar** across the top of the window displays the application name and the current open file. Underneath this is a **Menu Bar**, containing all the commands needed to control the application, grouped into drop down lists. Click the first menu item, **File**.

7. Click the chevrons, ⌄ , at the bottom of the menu to reveal all possible options. Take note of the available options, then browse through the other menu options.

8. Click on the white page area to remove the menus.

9. Underneath the **Menu Bar** should be two sets of toolbars, known as the **Standard** and **Formatting** bars. If either is not visible, then select **View | Toolbars** and make sure the relevant entries are selected (ticked).

   These toolbars may appear on a line each or appear in shortened form on the same line.

e-Citizen

© CiA Training Ltd 2004

10. Shortened toolbars are indicated by chevrons, [»]. Clicking the chevrons will reveal any buttons not currently available.

> *Several different toolbars may be displayed during specific functions or on request. These toolbars may appear at any edge of the screen or floating within the screen.*

11. Move the mouse pointer over any of the buttons on the toolbar, and leave it for a second or two. A **ScreenTip** appears, describing the button.

12. Leave *Word* open.

Entering, Formatting and Deleting Text

Word uses a flashing cursor to show the **Insertion Point** where the text will be entered. For a blank document, this will usually be in the top left corner. The insertion point moves as you type.

> The Insertion Point is indicated by a flashing cursor, to show where text will be entered. |
>
> *Insertion Point*

The cursor can be positioned anywhere in existing text by pointing and clicking with the mouse or using the keyboard cursor (arrow) keys. Any key pressed on the keyboard will appear in the document at the **Insertion Point**. Each letter, number or symbol typed is called a **character**.

Text is entered with automatic wordwrap, so that when the edge of the page is reached, the text automatically wraps on to the next line. Only press <**Enter**> if a new paragraph is to be started, or a new line is required before you reach the end of the current one. If a capital letter or a symbol at the top of a key, e.g. %, £, @, ?, is required, hold down the <**Shift**> key while typing it.

The appearance of text can be changed in a number of ways. This is known as **formatting**. Formatting can be chosen either before entering the text, or more commonly after entering text. The relevant text must be selected and then the formatting can be applied.

The font (the type of text, e.g. *Comic Sans MS*, **Impact**), style, size and colour of text can be changed in two ways. Either by selecting **Format | Font** and selecting from the dialog box, or by using the **Font**, [Times New Roman ▼] and **Font Size**, [10 ▼], drop down lists and the **Bold**,

B , Italic, *I* , Underline, **U** and Font Color, **A** buttons on the **Formatting Toolbar**. Some buttons may not be displayed, as the toolbars show only the most recently used buttons. When there is not enough room on the toolbar to display all of the available buttons, those that have not been used for a while are hidden. If you can't see a button, click the chevrons, » , at the right end of the toolbar to display the hidden buttons and then click on the one you need.

Exercise 13

1. Enter the following text into *Word*. Type carefully and accurately to try and avoid any mistakes. Press <**Enter**> twice after the end of the first paragraph, once to end the line and once to add a blank line.

> **Do you need help with IT? CiA Training Ltd is a specialist computer training company, based in the north east of England. It has been trading for over nineteen years and has recently moved to new, larger premises in Sunderland.**
>
> **The company is involved in training in all computer software applications and is also a major producer of Open Learning materials for computer software. More details are available by telephoning +44 (0) 191 549 5002. Alternatively, you can e-mail us at info@ciatraining.co.uk.**

2. Select the first sentence, **Do you need help with IT?** by clicking and dragging the mouse pointer over the text, so that it is highlighted (darker than the rest of the text), Do you need help with IT?.

3. Press the <**Delete**> key to remove the text.

4. To cancel the deletion, select **Edit | Undo Clear** from the menu (the wording after **Undo** changes to reflect the last action performed).

5. Click after **larger premises in Sunderland.** and type a new sentence: **These premises are located within the Business and Innovation Centre on the north bank of the River Wear.**

6. Hold down the <**Ctrl**> key then press <**A**>. The whole of the text will be selected.

7. Locate the **Font** drop down list, click and choose the **Arial** font. You may need to scroll to see it.

> (i) *If you are unfamiliar with these formatting terms, place the mouse pointer over the buttons on the **Formatting** toolbar and read each **ScreenTip** that appears.*

8. With the text still selected, click the drop down arrow on the **Font Size** list, `10 ▾` and choose **12** for the size, if it is not already selected.

9. Click in front of the second sentence and press <**Enter**> to move it on to a new line.

10. Select the first sentence again, by clicking and dragging.

11. Change the font of this sentence to **Comic Sans MS** (use the scroll bar at the right to see the font if necessary) and the **Font Size** to **16**.

12. Using the correct buttons, change the style of the selected text to **bold** and its colour to **red** and the alignment to **Center**. Alignment refers to the positioning of the text in relation to the margins.

13. Apply **Bold** and **Italic** to selected words in the text. An example of how the final document may look is shown below.

Do you need help with IT?

CiA Training Ltd is a *specialist computer training* company, based in the north east of England. It has been trading for over nineteen years and has recently moved to new, larger premises in Sunderland. These premises are located within the Business and Innovation Centre on the north bank of the River Wear.

The company is involved in training in all computer software applications and is also a major producer of *Open Learning materials* for computer software. More details are available by telephoning **+44 (0) 191 5495002**. Alternatively, you can e-mail us at **info@ciatraining.co.uk**.

---

14. Leave the document open for the next exercise.

Saving Work

The process used to save work is the same in most programs and it is important that you do save your work, otherwise it will be lost when you close the program. It is best to save a file (document, spreadsheet, etc.) as soon as you open it and at regular intervals while working.

There are two ways to save work.

A file can be saved by specifying a name, a location and a file type for the saved file. The **Save As** command displays a dialog box with these options. This process must be used to save new files.

An existing file can be saved using **Save As**, producing a new version of the file, or the **Save** command can be used to update the file, by saving it in the same location and with the same name as previously. This is a quicker process as it does not involve a dialog box.

If you use the **Save** command to save a new file, the **Save As** dialog box will be displayed automatically.

Exercise 14

1.   To save the new document, select **File | Save As**. The **Save As** dialog box will appear.

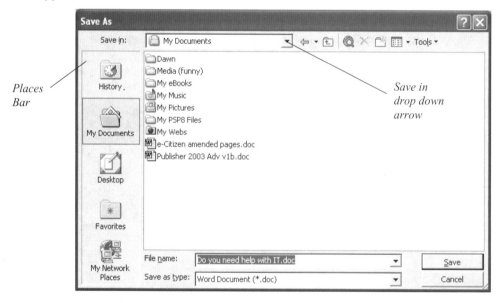

Places
Bar

Save in
drop down
arrow

ⓘ   *In the diagram above, file names are shown with extensions, e.g. **.doc**. This is a display option, which may not have been selected on your computer. This will be covered in Exercise 19.*

2.   The **Places Bar** can be used to specify the general area for saving. The **Save in** box at the top shows in detail the place where your work will be saved. This should be **My Documents**. Click the drop down arrow of **Save in** to see the locations where your file could be saved.

AT THE BOTTOM OF A SAVE AS DIALOG WINDOW

3. Click again to close the list. The white area of the dialog box shows all of the files and folders in **My Documents**, the **Save in** location.

   (i) *Double click any folder to make it the **Save in** location and display its contents.*

4. The document must have a name. Click in the **File name** box and highlight the existing name.

5. Enter **Typing** using the keyboard. The existing name is overwritten.

6. **Save as type** shows the format in which the document will be saved. By default, in *Word*, this is **Word Document (*.doc)**. Do not change this now.

7. Finally, to save the document, click the **Save** button, [<u>S</u>ave].

   (i) *So there are three things to remember when using **Save As**:*

   - ✓ *choose a place to save the file - **Save in***
   - ✓ *name the file - **File name***
   - ✓ *check the file type - **Save as type***

8. To be sure that your work has been saved, check the **Title Bar** at the top of *Word*, it should look like this, [**Typing.doc - Microsoft Word**].

9. Click and drag to select the first line of the document and use the **Font Color** drop down list, [**A** ▾] to change its colour from red to dark blue. Click away from the text to see the effect.

10. This change must be saved, or it will be lost when the program is closed. Click the **Save** button, [🖫]. There is no need to do anything else, the document will be saved with the existing name, replacing the original.

11. There are times when it is necessary to save a document as a different file type, for example if it is to be used in a different application. Select **File | Save As** and change the **File name** to **Training Web**.

12. Click the **Save as type** drop down arrow.

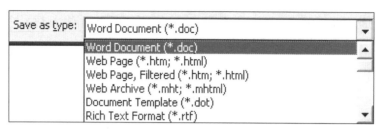

The file types shown above have file extensions displayed.

13. Browse through the list of available file formats, then select **Web Page (*.htm; *.html)**. This is a format that can be viewed on the Internet.

14. Make sure **Save in** shows **My Documents** and click **Save** to save the document as a web page.

15. Select **File | Save As** again and set the name to **Fancy** and the type as **Rich Text Format (*.rtf)**. This is a format that can be read by most applications, and can contain formatting such as bold or italic.

16. Click **Save**. The document will be saved as **Fancy.rtf**.

17. Select **File | Save As** again. This time select to save the document in **Plain Text (*.txt)** format (▦ *Text Only in Word 2000*), with the name **Simple**.

18. Click **Save** to save the document as **Simple.txt**, a plain text format with no formatting that can be read by most applications.

⬧ *If a warning about a loss of formatting appears, click **OK**.*

19. Highlight the first line of the document and delete it. Select **File | Close** to close the document. Because changes have been made since the last save there will be a prompt to save it now.

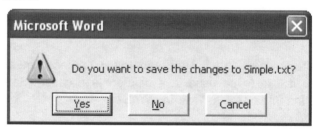

20. Click **Yes**. There may be another warning about losing formatting. Click **Yes** to continue. The file will be saved again and then closed.

Opening and Printing Documents

All office applications have the ability to open a file that has been saved previously, to amend it if required, and to obtain a printed copy (assuming a printer is connected to the computer).

It is an easy task to print out documents from *Word*. The printing margins can be set from the **Page Setup** dialog box. The page layout can be previewed before printing in **Print Preview**, where a picture of the printed page will appear, along with the margins that have been set. A choice of printer can be made if more than one is available.

It is possible to print documents without opening them, even directly from a floppy disk or CD. When a file anywhere on your computer is listed in the **My Computer** window, right clicking on the file name will produce a shortcut menu with several options. If the file is capable of being printed, there will be a **Print** option. Clicking the print option will print one copy of the selected file to the default printer.

Exercise 15

1. Any saved document can be easily opened in *Word*. With *Word* open but no documents displayed, select **File | Open** or click the **Open** button, 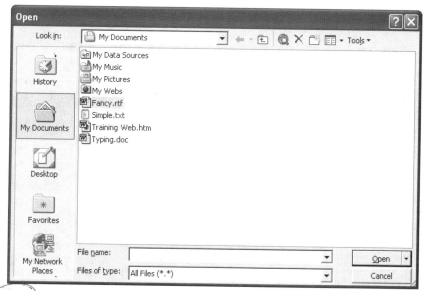.

2. The **Open** dialog box is displayed, which is similar in layout to the **Save As** dialog box. Make sure the **Look in** box shows the location of the recently saved files, and

Files of type shows **All Files.** If the correct location is <u>not</u> shown, click the drop down arrow at the right of **Look in** and select it. If **All Files** is <u>not</u> displayed, click the drop down arrow at the right of **Files of type** and select it.

3. Select **Typing.doc** from the list of files and click **Open**, [Open ▾]. The document is displayed.

4. Click the **Print Preview** button, to display an image of how the printed document will look.

5. The cursor becomes over the page image. Click to zoom into the image. Click again to zoom out.

6. Click [Close] to close **Print Preview**.

7. Select **File | Page Setup** to display the **Page Setup** dialog box.

8. Examine the various options under each of the tabs of the dialog box. The most common settings made here are to vary the margin widths (under **Margins**), and set portrait, [A], or landscape, [A], orientation (▦ *under Paper Size in Word 2000*).

9. Click **Cancel** to close the dialog box without making any changes.

10. Switch on your printer and make sure it is loaded with paper.

11. Select **File | Print** to display the **Print** dialog box.

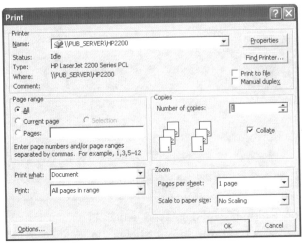

> (i) *If more than one printer is available to your computer, you can select the required printer from the **Printer Name** drop down list. The printing options available may vary for different printers.*

12. Examine the options available for **Page range**. There are options to print the entire document, the current page only, or a specific set of page numbers. These options are useful when dealing with large documents. Change the setting to **Current page**.

13. In the **Copies** area set the **Number of copies** to **2**.

14. Click **OK** and two copies of the current page of the document will print.

> (i) *Alternatively, to print one copy of the whole document on the default printer without showing the dialog box, click the **Print** button,* 🖨.

15. Close the document, using **File | Close**.

16. Leave *Word* open for the next exercise.

Closing an Application

More than one application can be running within *Windows* at one time, although only one will be the active application. To finish using an application and clear it from *Windows*, it must be closed. There are various methods to close down an active application.

Exercise 16

1. With *Word* still open, select **Start** from the **Taskbar** and select **All Programs | Accessories | Calculator**.

2. The **Calculator** window will open without closing *Word*. Look at the **Taskbar**. It shows two buttons, representing two open tasks.

3. The active window is shown by a coloured **Title Bar** on the window and by its **Taskbar** button appearing to be darker.

4. Click the **Taskbar** button for the *Word* application. It now becomes active (it may completely hide the calculator window).

5. Make the calculator the active window again then click the **Close** button, ⊠, at the top right of its **Title Bar**. The calculator application will be closed and removed from the **Taskbar**.

6. Click anywhere in the *Word* window to make it the active application.

7. As an alternative way to close the application, select **File | Exit**. *Word* is closed and its button removed from the **Taskbar**.

Exercise 17 - Revision: Simple Applications

1. The application used to create a word processed document is:

    a) *Excel*

    b) *Word*

    c) *PowerPoint*

    d) *Windows*

2. Which format would you use to save a word processed document, so the document could be opened in other word processing applications?

    a) **.doc** format

    b) **.htm** format

    c) **.rtf** format

    d) **.xls** format

3. When saving a document in *Word*, what is the default file location?

    a) **My Data Sources**

    b) **My Music**

    c) **My Webs**

    d) **My Documents**

4. Having created a document, what would you use to save an updated version of the same document with a different name?

   a) The **Save** button, ✓

   b) The menu **File | Save**

   c) The menu **File | Save As**

   d) Type the document again and use any method to save it with the required name

5. Which three properties must be specified when saving a new file from a word processing application?

   a) Size, Name and File Type

   b) Location, Name and File Type ✓

   c) Location, Name and Size

   d) Location, Size and Date

   ⓘ *Answers are listed in the **Answers Section** at the end of the guide.*

Chapter 3 - Files and Folders

In this chapter you will learn how to: understand the structure of files and folders on a computer, use **Folders View**, recognise file types, create new folders, copy, move and delete files and folders, use the **Recycle Bin**, use **Help**.

File Storage

Computers store their data and programs on a variety of **Storage Devices**, from where it is transferred into active memory for processing when required. Unlike memory, these storage devices retain data even when the power is removed. The vast majority of computers have a **Hard Disk Drive** (HDD), the main storage device for the system, which is usually referred to as drive **C**. It is possible however to have further such drives installed, which would then become drive **D**, etc. The **Hard Disk Drive** can store a vast amount of data, which can be accessed very quickly.

Most computers also have a **Floppy Disk Drive**, which stores and retrieves data using removable diskettes. These are used to transfer or store relatively small amounts of data. The floppy disk drive is referred to as drive **A**.

A **Compact Disk Drive** uses compact disks (CDs) to store data; each CD holds about 500 times more information than a floppy disk. Some drives will only read from existing CDs, others (CD writers) allow data to be written on to a blank CD. CD devices are assigned drive letters after the last hard disk drive, so if your hard disk drive is **C**, the CD drive will be **D**.

In the rapidly changing world of computer hardware, new and better storage devices are being developed on a regular basis. For example, DVD drives are available which operate on similar principles to CD storage but with greatly increased capacity. Also small solid state memory devices called Flash Drives are becoming increasingly popular.

Exercise 18

1. With the *Windows* **Desktop** displayed, double click on the **My Computer** icon, to open that window and display the storage devices available on your computer.

2.   If the display is not in this form, select **View | Icons**.

> ▦ *In **Windows 2000**, icons are displayed in a continuous row. Select **View | Large Icons**.*

3.   This is the display for a typical system and may be different on other computers. A hand symbol in the **Shared Documents** icon indicates that this resource may be shared by other computers on the network. Look to see if one is present on the display.

4.   Find the description **Local Disk** beneath one of the icons. This term implies that the drive is physically located in this computer, rather than a shared drive in another computer.

> ⓘ *The contents of any device can be displayed by double clicking the icon.*

5.   Close **My Computer**.

Folders and Files

In order to assist in storing and finding files and programs on a computer, *Windows* uses **Folders**. Any storage device, hard disk, floppy disk, or CD, can be split into many folders, each containing all the files related to a specific task or program. A folder may also contain other folders, called subfolders. The concept is much like organising a filing cabinet by having separate drawers and files for each particular task. A folder containing subfolders is sometimes called a **directory**.

A folder in *Windows* appears as an icon,  , with the name of the folder printed next to or underneath it, depending on the view displayed. When the icon is double clicked, the folder opens, and its contents are displayed in the window.

Exercise 19

1. Double click on **My Documents** on the **Desktop** to open the **My Documents** folder and display the files contained in it.

2. Select **View | Details** to see the files listed with more information.

3. If the 3-character file extensions are not displayed after the file names, select **Tools | Folder Options** and click on the **View** tab. Make sure that the **Hide file extensions for known file types** is <u>unchecked</u>. Click **OK** to display the file extensions. The **Name** column may have to be expanded (click and drag between the column headings) to the right to display more file name information.

4. There are at least 4 files displayed - those created in the previous chapter. These represent 4 different types of files. The **.doc** is a *Word* document, the **.txt** is a basic text file, the **.rtf** is a rich text format file and the **.htm** is a web page. File types are covered in more detail in a later exercise.

5. Close the **My Documents** window using the **Close** button, ❎, at the top right of the window.

Folders View

Folders View displays the organisation of files and folders in any open window. It shows the storage of data on a computer in a hierarchical way. This means that it will show the main devices available to the computer, then each device can be expanded to show the component folders and files, and each folder can be further expanded down to the lowest possible level.

It can also be used to control the copying, moving, creating and deleting of files and folders, known as **File Management**. In previous versions of *Windows*, e.g. *98*, this function was carried out using *Windows Explorer*. This program is still available and can be found under **Accessories**.

Exercise 20

1. From the **Desktop** open the **My Computer** window and make sure it is displayed as a full screen. Use the **Maximise** button if necessary.

2. Click the **Folders** button, [Folders], on the toolbar to display the **Folders** pane. All storage devices will be listed there under **My Computer**.

3. Click once on **Local Disk (C:)** in the **Folders** pane, to display its contents in the **View Pane** on the right. Select **View | Details**.

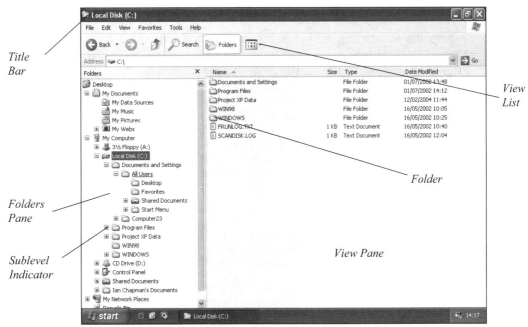

Title Bar

Folders Pane

Sublevel Indicator

View List

Folder

View Pane

> The contents will be different to that above. There are also different views of the same information. The window above is viewed showing **Details**.

4.   On the left is the **Folders pane**, which shows the drives and folders on the computer. On the right is the **View pane**, showing the contents of the selected drive or folder. Scroll through the list of drives and folders in the **Folders pane**.

5.   Click on any folder icon in the **Folders pane**. The contents of the folder are shown in the **View pane**.

6.   Select **View | Icons**. The contents are now shown as small icons.

7.   Select **View | Details**. The folder contents now have their name, size, type and date modified shown. This enables the smallest, largest, newest, oldest and files of the same type to be identified. Different types of file are displayed with a different icon before the name.

8.   In the **Folders pane**, locate **My Documents** (at the top, just below **Desktop**), it has a ⊞ icon in front of it, meaning that the folder has subfolders. Click once on ⊞, the subfolders are displayed underneath the main folder and the icon changes to a ⊟ icon. This is called **expanding** a folder.

9.   Expand any folder.

10. To hide the subfolders, click the ⊟ icon next to expanded folders. The ⊟ icon changes to a ⊞ icon again and the subfolders or files are hidden. This is called **collapsing** a folder.

11. Expand the same folder again and then click once on a subfolder to display the files in it. Make sure **View** is set to **Details**.

Name ▲	Size	Type	Date Modified
Array.xls	15 KB	Microsoft Excel Worksheet	17/06/2004 13:41
Bus.jpg	19 KB	JPEG Image	16/06/2004 09:22
Ciasupport.htm	35 KB	HTML Document	01/09/2004 09:54
Carafe.bmp	13 KB	Bitmap Image	16/06/2004 09:22
Doc1.doc	104 KB	Microsoft Word Document	22/07/2004 15:15
Egypt.mdb	2,012 KB	Microsoft Office Access Application	04/08/2004 16:34
Egyptian.avi	1,378 KB	Video Clip	16/06/2004 09:22
Internet.doc	27 KB	Microsoft Word Document	21/06/2004 15:17
meeting.gif	11 KB	GIF Image	22/06/2004 16:17
movie.mpeg	399 KB	Movie File (MPEG)	05/09/2001 13:26
Results.xls	14 KB	Microsoft Excel Worksheet	17/06/2004 13:39
Sound.wav	32 KB	Wave Sound	02/02/1999 18:55
Teams.txt	1 KB	Text Document	29/06/2004 09:09
test1.pdf	1,004 KB	Adobe Acrobat Document	28/06/2004 15:43
Training.ppt	91 KB	Microsoft PowerPoint Presentation	07/04/2004 15:04

Sample folder contents showing a variety of different file types.

e-Citizen
© CiA Training Ltd 2004

File Types

File types are represented by a dot and a 3 (or 4) character file extension after a file name and tell the computer system what type of file it is. When a file is created by an application, e.g. spreadsheet, the correct file extension is automatically added.

Care should be taken when copying or renaming files to maintain the correct file extension. Changing the file extension does not change the file contents, but will confuse the computer operating system. For example, if a spreadsheet file is given a **.doc** extension and then double clicked, *Word* will attempt to open it and there will be an error.

Some file types are software independent, e.g. **.txt** and **.rtf**, as mentioned earlier.

Word processed documents can usefully be saved as rich text format files (**.rtf**) since this retains some of their basic formatting, while allowing them to be opened by any word processing application.

Some common file types are listed here:

Extension	Icon	Description
.doc		*Word* document
.mdb		*Access* database
.ppt		*PowerPoint* presentation
.xls		*Excel* spreadsheet
.htm		Web page
.avi, **.mpeg**		Video files
.exe		Executable file, i.e. a program
.jpg, **.tif**, **.gif**, **.bmp**	,	Graphic/image files
.tmp	or	Temporary file. One used by the system during a process and then deleted automatically
.txt, **.rtf**		Generic text files
.wav, **.mp3**		Audio or sound files
.zip	or	A compressed (zipped) archive file

Exercise 21

1. Click on the **My Documents** folder and, in **Details** view, identify each of the file types in the folder just by the icon and the file extension.

2. Click on the **Type** heading (see picture on page 55) to group the files by type. Now click on the **Name** heading to list the files alphabetically.

Creating New Folders

New folders are created to organise your files and keep files relating to a similar subject together. The **File | New | Folder** command is used to create new folders. Folders created within other folders are called **subfolders**.

Exercise 22

1. Ensure that the **My Documents** folder is selected. The contents of this folder are now displayed in the **View pane**, on the right.

2. To create a subfolder in the selected folder, **My Documents**, select **File | New | Folder**. The newly created folder appears in the **View** window. It is highlighted, ready for the name to be entered, New Folder .

3. Type in **Working Files** as a name for the folder.

4. Press <**Enter**> to complete the process. The folder is now created and named.

5. Click the **Working Files** folder in the **Folders Pane** on the left and create a folder within the **Working Files** folder.

6. Name the subfolder **Internet Files**.

7. Click on the ⊞ next to the **Working Files** folder to see the newly created **Internet Files** subfolder within it.

8. Click on the subfolder **Internet Files** to show its contents in the **View Pane** on the right; it is empty.

Copying Files and Folders

Selected files or folders can be copied in a variety of ways: by dragging from one location to another using the left or right mouse button or by using the copy and paste commands.

Objects can be copied between locations on the same drive or from one drive to another. Copying important files from the hard disk to a different drive, usually a floppy or CD, is known as creating a backup. These backup copies will be invaluable if the original data is ever lost or corrupted, due to virus action, accidental deletion or hard disk failure, for example. In this exercise, you will copy between folders on the same drive, **C**.

Exercise 23

1. Click on the **My Documents** folder in the **Folders** pane. The contents of this folder are now displayed in the **View** window. Notice how the files you created in the previous chapter are all there.

2. Hold down the <**Ctrl**> key and click and drag the file **Typing.doc** across to the **Working Files** folder in the **Folders** pane. Notice that the mouse pointer has a plus sign next to it, this means that the file is being copied, rather than moved.

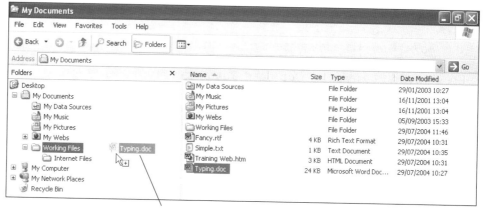

*The file **Typing.doc** being copied to the **Working Files** folder.*

3. Release the mouse button and then the <**Ctrl**> key. As the file was dragged with the <**Ctrl**> key held down, it was copied.

> *When copying to or from a different drive, e.g. the floppy disk (usually drive **A:**) or CD (often drive **D:**) there is no need to hold down <**Ctrl**> as you drag.*

 *Writing to a CD requires that you have a CD drive capable of writing, and earlier versions of Windows require the use of special software.*

4. Repeat this process to copy the **Simple.txt** file to the **Working Files** folder.

5. Click on the **Working Files** folder to check that it contains a subfolder, **Internet Files,** and two files as below.

Internet Files

Simple.txt
Text Document
1 KB

Typing.doc
Microsoft Word Document
24 KB

6. View the contents of **My Documents**.

7. Another and much safer method to copy files uses the right mouse button. Click and drag the **Fancy.rtf** icon to the **Working Files** folder using the right mouse button. Release the mouse button.

> Copy Here
> **Move Here**
> Create Shortcuts Here
>
> Cancel

8. Select **Copy Here** from the shortcut menu to copy the file.

9. The **Edit** commands, **Copy** and **Paste**, can also be used to copy files. Copying within the same folder produces a duplicate copy of a file. View the contents of the folder **My Documents**. Click on the **Training Web.htm** file, then from the menu select **Edit | Copy**. Select **Edit | Paste** to create a **Copy of Training Web.htm** in the same folder.

Copy of Training Web.htm   4 KB   HTML Document   09/03/2004 09:34

10. Files can easily be renamed. Click on the above file to select it then select **File | Rename**. Type in a new name of **Training Backup.htm**, which will replace the original name. Press **<Enter>** to complete the name change.

> *It is important to include the same file extension when renaming files otherwise applications will not be able to correctly identify the type of file.*

11. Use either method to copy **Training Web.htm** from **My Documents** to the **Internet Files** folder.

12. Use **Copy** and **Paste** to produce a copy of the **Typing** file in **My Documents**.

13. Rename the copied file **Copy of Typing.doc** as **Typing2.doc**.

14. Folders are copied in the same way as files. In the **View Pane**, select the **Internet Files** subfolder within your **Working Files** folder.

15. Use any of the methods already shown to copy the **Internet Files** folder to **My Documents**.

> *Copying folders to the same location as described above is only done as an example in this guide. Usually folders are copied to and from removable media, e.g. floppy disk or CD, in order to create a backup of the original content.*

16. Click on **My Documents** in the **Folders Pane** on the left. Click on the **Internet Files** folder in the **View Pane** on the right.

17. Select **File | Rename** and change the name of the folder to **Backup Files**. Press <**Enter**>.

18. Leave the window open.

Moving Files and Folders

Moving a file or folder is a similar process to copying. A file or folder can be moved from one location to another on the same drive by dragging and dropping using the left mouse button. Hold down **Shift** while dragging if you are moving objects to a different drive. Alternatively the **Move To** or **Cut** and **Paste** commands could be used to move objects to any location, or use click and drag with the **right** mouse button and select **Move Here** from the shortcut menu when the button is released.

Exercise 24

1. Display the files within the **My Documents** folder.

2. Expand the folder to display the **Working Files** and **Internet Files** subfolders.

3. In the **View Pane**, click and drag the file icon **Typing2.doc** towards the **Working Files** folder. Notice that the cursor has no ⊞ icon, indicating that the file is going to be *moved*, then release the mouse button when over the **Working Files** folder.

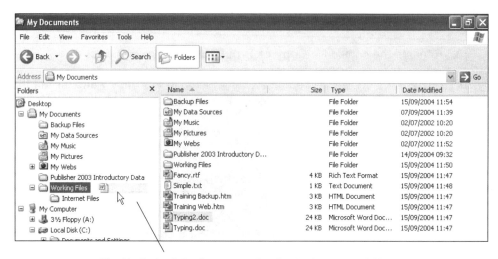

*The file **Typing2.doc** being moved to the **Working Files** folder.*

4. Check in the **View Pane** that the file **Typing2.doc** has been removed from the **My Documents** window.

5. Open the **Working Files** folder. The **Typing2.doc** icon is displayed, with **Typing.doc**, **Fancy.rtf** and **Simple.txt**, copied there in the previous exercise.

6. Display the contents of the **My Documents** folder.

7. Using the right mouse, click and drag the **Training Backup.htm** icon from the **My Documents** folder to the **Internet Files** folder button. Release the mouse button.

8. Select **Move Here** from the shortcut menu to move the file.

9. When a file is copied or moved to a location which already contains a file of the same name, there is an option to replace the original file with the new one. Use any method to move **Simple.txt** from **My Documents** to the **Working Files** subfolder.

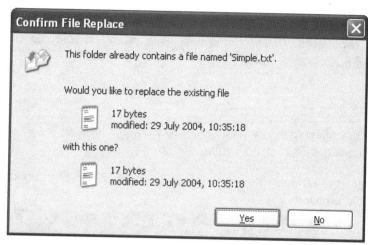

10. Select **Yes** to replace the existing file.

11. Use any method to move **Fancy.rtf** from **My Documents** to the **Working Files** subfolder.

Deleting Files and Folders

Files and folders can be deleted in four main ways:

- Select the icon by clicking it, then press the <**Delete**> key.

- Click once on the file / folder with the right mouse button then select **Delete**.

- Click and drag the file / folder over the **Recycle Bin** icon on the **Desktop** or in **Folders view**, Recycle Bin , then release the icon "into" the bin.

- Select the file and click on the **Delete** button, X on the toolbar.

When files or folders are deleted, they are not instantly removed from the hard disk. They are held in the **Recycle Bin**, whose icon can be seen on the **Desktop** or in any **Folders** pane. All deleted items are stored there until the **Recycle Bin** is emptied. Until then, the files can be restored to their original location.

*The result of deleting files depends on where the files are located. If the file is on a hard disk, then the file is removed (after a confirmation prompt), and placed in the **Recycle Bin**. If the file is on a floppy disk, a message appears checking if the user is sure that the file is to be deleted, as it will be deleted permanently.*

Once the **Recycle Bin** is emptied, the contents are **permanently** deleted and **can no longer be recovered**. Deleting individual items from the **Recycle Bin** also permanently removes them.

Exercise 25

1. In the **View** pane, make sure the contents of the **My Documents** folder are displayed, then click on **Typing.doc** to select it.

2. Press the <**Delete**> key. A message appears, requesting confirmation that the file is to be removed.

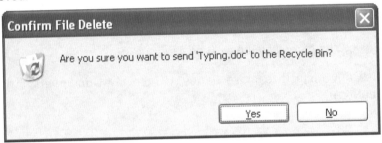

3. Click **Yes** to move the file to the **Recycle Bin**. The icon disappears from the **My Documents** window and the file is deleted by moving it to the **Recycle Bin**.

4. Deleting folders is the same as deleting files. Delete the **Working Files** folder, including the **Internet Files** subfolder and files, from **My Documents** using the **Delete** key.

5. When a folder is deleted, a **Confirm Folder Delete** message may be displayed. If so, click **Yes** to delete the folder by moving it and all its contents to the **Recycle Bin**.

6. Delete the **Backup Files** folder from **My Documents**.

    *To retrieve an item from the **Recycle Bin**, click the **Recycle Bin** icon in any **Folders** pane to display its contents, a list of all items that have been deleted. To restore a file or a folder, right click on it and select **Restore** to remove the file from the **Recycle Bin** and place it where it was before deletion (missing folders will be recreated where necessary).*

    *To empty the **Recycle Bin**, click with the **right** mouse button on the **Recycle Bin** icon on the **Desktop** or within **Folders** view. From the shortcut menu, select **Empty Recycle Bin**. A message appears confirming the action.*

7. Check that you still have the **Training Web.htm** file in the **My Documents** folder.

8. Close any open windows.

Using Help

Windows has a built in **Help** facility to assist the user when information is required. There are many different ways of accessing the **Help** content.

All individual office applications, such as word processing and spreadsheet applications, will have their own built in Help facilities, with content appropriate to their function.

Exercise 26

1. Click the **Start** button and select **Help and Support**.

    *This option was named **Help** in earlier versions of Windows.*

2. Extra Help information is available online from the *Microsoft Support* site and there may be a prompt at this stage to connect to the Internet (if you are not already connected). It is not necessary to be online to complete this exercise.

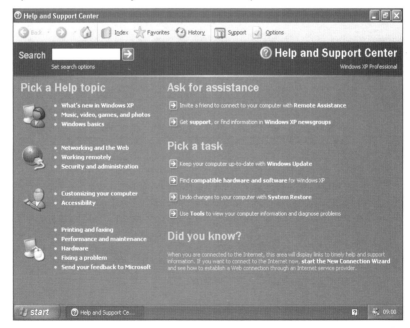

*The **Windows 2000** help dialog box has four tabs, **Contents**, **Index**, **Search** and **Favorites**, instead of the options shown on the previous page. Click on the required tab to see options for locating **Help**.*

3. Move the mouse over each of the text links in the toolbar to display a **ScreenTip** about the button's function.

4. Click the **Index** button, [Index], on the toolbar. **Index** gives an alphabetic list of every available help topic and can be searched using the scroll bar. The required topic can also be quickly found by entering it in the box above the list.

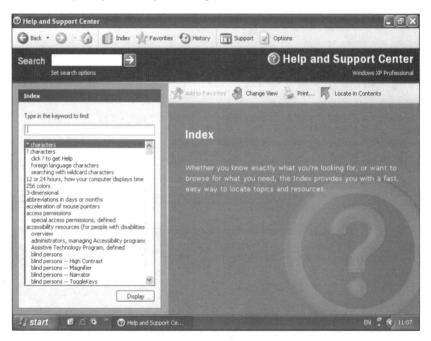

5. Using the scroll bar, move down the list until **adjusting volume** is visible. Click on this topic, then click **Display** to see the help on the right.

*In **Windows 2000** choose the **system sound volume** subentry from below **adjusting volume** before clicking **Display**.*

6. With the **Index** still open, click in the **Type in the keyword to find** box, delete the contents and enter the word **taskbar**.

7. In the topic list below, under the topic **taskbar** click on **hiding**.

e-Citizen
© CiA Training Ltd 2004

8. Click the **Display** button and **Help** is displayed on the right.

> ⊞ *Windows 2000 users omit steps 9-15.*

9. Click the **Home** button, [🏠], to return to the **Help and Support** window.

10. The **Search** box just under the toolbar can also be used to find help. Type **printer drivers** in the **Search** box and click **Start searching**, [→].

11. From **Search Results**, click on **Printer drivers overview** and read the help at the right.

12. Click the **Home** button again to return to the **Help and Support** window.

13. Help can be accessed in a more general way by using the **Topics**. Click **What's new in Windows XP**.

14. Click [+] at the left of **Windows components**. Click **Accessories** and from the right of the window click **Using Paint**.

15. Read the help text then close the **Help and Support Center** window by clicking its **Close** button, [✕].

16. Select the **Start** button and then **Control Panel**. The **Control Panel** contains many tools used for configuring and changing the way *Windows* looks and acts.

> ⊞ *In Windows 2000 select Start | Settings | Control Panel.*

17. Double click on the **Display** icon to open the **Display Properties** dialog box and make sure the **Settings** tab is selected.

18. The dialog box has a help symbol, [?], at the top right which means there is context specific help available. Click the help symbol. The cursor changes to ⍰?.

19. Move this cursor over the **Screen resolution** area and click to display help text specific to that item.

> ⊞ *In Windows 2000 Screen resolution is Screen area.*

> Displays the current screen resolution settings for the monitor whose video adapter appears in **Display**. Drag the slider to specify the screen resolution you want. As you increase the number of pixels, you display more information on your screen, but the information decreases in size.

*An alternative method of displaying this specific help text is to right click on a feature of the dialog box and click the **What's This** option that appears.*

20. Click anywhere to remove the help text.

21. Display specific help text for other areas of the dialog box.

22. Close the **Display Properties** dialog box by clicking **Cancel**.

23. Close the **Control Panel**.

Exercise 27 - Revision: Files and Folders

1. A **folder** is:

    a) An area in a filing cabinet

    b) A named location for storing files

    c) A word processed document

    d) An origami expert

2. Which of the following terms <u>best</u> describes **File Management**?

    a) The copying and moving of files

    b) The copying, moving, creating and deleting of files and folders

    c) A method of keeping your files in one place

    d) A method of saving your work

3. In the diagram of a file structure below, are the following statements true or false?

a) **Quality** is a sub folder of **Health and Safety**

b) **Equal Opportunities Policy** is a file

c) **Grievance Records** is a folder

d) **Quality** is a file

e) **Health and Safety** is a sub folder of **Company Documents**

4. If a file is dragged from one location to another location on the same drive, which of the following statements is true?

a) The file is copied

b) The file is deleted

c) The file is moved

d) The action will have no effect on the file

5. Which of the following statements are true and which are false?

a) Every deleted file goes into the **Recycle Bin**

b) A file in the **Recycle Bin** can be restored

c) A file in the **Recycle Bin** cannot be restored if the folder of origin has been deleted

d) Files deleted from a floppy disk cannot be restored

ⓘ *Answers are listed in the **Answers Section** at the end of the guide.*

Chapter 4 - Internet Basics

In this chapter you will learn how to: understand Internet principles, use Internet Explorer, navigate using web addresses and hyperlinks, use a search engine.

Internet Principles

What is the Internet?

The **Internet** is a vast computer network, which allows users all over the world to communicate with each other. The **World Wide Web** (www) is not the same thing as the Internet; it is the collection of information that can be accessed via the Internet. This information is stored on the web in web sites (web pages) each of which has a unique address. Multi-page sites usually contain a **Home Page**, consisting of an introduction to the site and often containing links to other pages on that site. Many sites also contain links to different related sites. It is because any site can be linked to many other related sites, each one of which in turn will be linked to many more, that led to the idea of a huge web of information (the world wide web).

e-Participation

The Internet can be used to find information on almost any subject The interconnected mass of information can be browsed relatively simply, by choosing a trail of links from one site to another. More and more, as an alternative to conventional shopping, the Internet is being used to purchase goods. Services such as online banking, health insurance and even education can be accessed in this way. As the Internet has no international boundaries, users can interact with sites throughout the world, from local councils and medical centres, to multinational companies and organisations. Users can now participate and make their voices heard in a range of areas; this would have been impossible only a few years ago.

How do I connect?

Connections to the Internet are made via an **Internet Service Provider** (**ISP**). These are organisations that provide a powerful computer with the necessary technology to connect efficiently to the Internet. Users then connect to the ISP computer via some kind of telephone connection (dial up or broadband) and the ISP computer handles the flow of data between individual users and the Internet. Your own computer must have a suitable connection and a **modem** (converts digital and analogue signals so the computer can connect to the telephone/cable line) before the Internet can be accessed. To summarise then, the requirements for Internet access are: a personal computer, a modem, a connection to the telephone network, and an account with an ISP. Once connected, a browser is normally used to provide the interface between the user and the World Wide Web.

What is a browser?

Software applications called **browsers** are used to make it easy to display and control the information available from the World Wide Web. These applications handle the initial connection to the ISP, make it easy to move from site to site, keep records of recently visited sites, and allow a folder of favourite sites to be maintained for easy access.

 *This guide has been written assuming that **Internet Explorer** is the browser in use, and all screen shots and options reflect this. Other browsers will however follow the same principles.*

What else will an Internet connection give me?

Most ISPs will also provide an **e-mail account**, an identifiable area on their computer for you to send and receive electronic communications to and from other Internet users. An application on your computer, e.g. *Microsoft Outlook Express* will allow you to access this area using a supplied ID and password.

Are there any pitfalls?

All this information and potential does have its price however. It is impossible to completely regulate such a huge international network and there are considerable security implications. These include misuse of personal information obtained from your computer, and unauthorised transmission of items such as viruses, to your computer. These topics are covered in a later chapter.

Exercise 28

Match the term in the first column with the definition in the second.

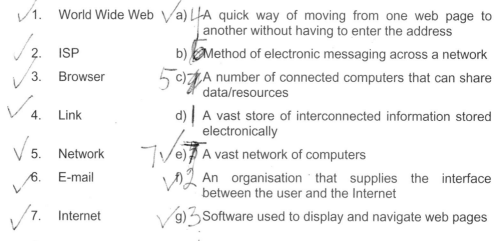

1. World Wide Web
2. ISP
3. Browser
4. Link
5. Network
6. E-mail
7. Internet

a) A quick way of moving from one web page to another without having to enter the address

b) Method of electronic messaging across a network

c) A number of connected computers that can share data/resources

d) A vast store of interconnected information stored electronically

e) A vast network of computers

f) An organisation that supplies the interface between the user and the Internet

g) Software used to display and navigate web pages

(i) *Answers are listed in the **Answers Section** at the end of the guide.*

Internet Explorer

When *Internet Explorer* is started and a connection to the Internet is active, a page from a web site will be displayed. This first page displayed is called your home page.

Exercise 29

1. Select **start** from the *Windows* **Desktop**.

2. Select the **Internet Explorer** icon from the left of the **Start Menu**. If there is not a connection to the Internet currently active, and automatic dialling has not been set in your **Internet Properties** settings, you will be prompted to make a connection.

▦ *Select **Start** / **Programs** / **Internet Explorer**, to start the application.*

Alternatively, double click *on the **Desktop** or single click* *on the* ***Taskbar**.*

 If you have a cable broadband connection it is always connected to the Internet, so you won't have to go through the connection process. The connection dialog box for an ADSL (through a telephone line) broadband connection may look different, but is, in principle, the same.

3. Click **Connect**, and a **Dial-up Connection** dialog box will be displayed. As well as the default *Windows* dialog box, many **ISPs** provide their own version of the connection process with their own start-up icon and connection dialog box.

Windows Connection Box.   *ISP specific Connection Box (Demon).*

4. The **User name** and **Password** will usually be shown. If not, enter the relevant **User name** and **Password**. Click on **Connect** (or **Dial**, depending on the dialog box).

5. Once the connection is made, your default **Home Page** will be displayed in the *Internet Explorer* window.

 Shaded boxes as above are used to denote steps in exercises that involve uncontrolled access to the Internet. The web sites visited are real and therefore care should be taken with these parts of the exercises.

Menu Bar

Toolbar

Address Bar

View Window

Status Bar

Links Bar

Scroll Bar

ⓘ *The Microsoft News site (**www.msn.com**) is shown here as the default home page. The actual page content is not relevant at this stage.*

6.   Examine the page and identify the following parts:

Menu Bar   containing a variety of drop down commands where selections are made

Toolbar   containing a series of icons which perform the most common commands

Address Bar   displaying the address of the web site being viewed

Links Bar   providing a way of getting to another web page

View window   displaying the actual web page

Status Bar   showing the user exactly what *Internet Explorer* is doing

Scroll Bar   at the far right of the screen, allowing the user to move up and down the page, if necessary

7.   Select **View | Toolbars | Customize**.

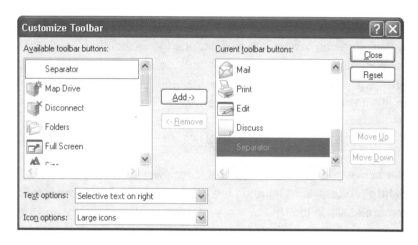

8. Select each of the **Text options** values and see how the toolbar buttons change,

e.g. . Select **Selective text on right** and click **Close**.

Web Addresses

Every web site on the Internet has its own unique address (like every telephone has a unique number on the telephone network). The simplest way of visiting a web site is by entering a form of this address, the **URL** (**Universal Resource Locator**), in the **Address Bar** of the browser. It is important to ensure that the exact address is entered. The sheer volume of sites on the World Wide Web means that changing a single character may well access another, irrelevant, site.

The **URL** for a site is made up of four main segments:

The first represents the **protocol** used by the site. A protocol is a set of rules that determine how computers transfer data between one another. All web sites use the protocol **http** (**Hypertext Transfer Protocol**) so *Internet Explorer* automatically enters (http://), to start every web address.

The next part of the address represents the general location of the site and is normally **www** to indicate that the site is part of the **World Wide Web**.

Then comes the specific name of the site. This often is the name of the company, etc. who own the site, but because each site name must be unique, sometimes invented names must be used.

The final part is the domain name, e.g. **.com**, which indicates the broad classification of the site. The domain name can be sub-divided, often to include the identity of the country where the server is located, e.g. **.au** for Australia and **.de** for Germany. Some web addresses have extensions, e.g. **.gov.uk** to indicate a government department, **.ac.uk** to indicate an educational establishment such as a university, or **.org** to indicate a charity.

Taking the above address as an example, **http://www.ciasupport.co.uk**, indicates that the site uses **http** protocol, is situated on the **World Wide Web**, has a name of **ciasupport**, and is a **Commercial** site in the **UK**.

Every web site has a **Home Page**. There is a difference between the **Home Page** of a site, which is the first page to appear when the site is opened and your **Home Page**, which is the

page loaded by the browser when it starts, or when you click the **Home** button, .

Exercise 30

1. Click in the **Address Bar** of the browser screen and enter the following address: **www.ciasupport.co.uk** (the address of our support web site) then press <**Enter**> or click .

2. The site home page for **ciasupport** will be displayed. Read the text on the page, then in the **Address Bar** highlight the text already there and type **www.disney.go.com** and press <**Enter**>. A small pop up window may appear as the page loads; it can either be closed or ignored.

> ⓘ   *If the page required is that of a large company, it may be possible to find it by typing just the name, e.g.* **Disney** *in the* **Address Bar***.*

3. Read some of the text on this page then type **www.bbc.co.uk** in the **Address Bar** and press <**Enter**>.

4. With the **BBC** page displayed, click the **Back** button, on the **Toolbar**. The previous page in the sequence of visited pages is displayed.

5. Click **Back** again to move to the **ciasupport** site.

6. Click **Back** again to return to your home page. The **Back** button becomes ghosted (pale grey). This means that the first page viewed in this session has been reached.

7. Now click the **Forward** button, . *Internet Explorer* will move forward to the next page in the sequence.

8. Continue pressing the **Forward** button to move forward through the pages until the **Forward** button is ghosted. This indicates that the most recent page in the sequence is displayed (the BBC page) and it is not possible to go further forward.

9. Click the arrow to the right of the **Back** button to reveal a drop down list of all sites in this current sequence.

10. Click any one to go to it directly.

11. Click the small black arrow to the right of the **Address Bar** button to reveal a drop down list of all sites visited recently.

12. Find the entry for the **BBC** site and click on it. The page is displayed.

13. Click to return to your home page and leave it open.

Using Hyperlinks

Another easy way to access different web pages is using **hyperlinks**, sometimes referred to simply as **links**. These are pieces of coloured text, pictures or buttons which have a URL coded within them.

A single click on a hyperlink and you are transferred immediately to a different site, or a different page or a different part of the same page, within the current site.

Each text line on the following diagram is a link to a new page within the web site, so the whole site is accessible from this one location.

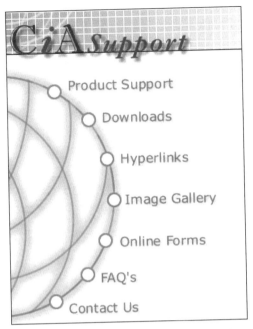

The advantage of using hyperlinks to navigate within the pages of a single site is that they make it much more user-friendly to navigate.

The more common use of hyperlinks is to link to other sites. There is no limit to the number of hyperlinks a web site can have. As any site can be linked to many other related sites, each one of which in turn will be linked to many more, it is possible to browse through the sites of the world wide web using only hyperlinks. Links to new areas can be uncovered and you may find yourself on a path far removed from the original query. This process is sometimes referred to as **surfing the web**.

Exercise 31

1. Use any method to display the **ciasupport** site, e.g. the drop down arrow on the **Address Bar**. If a new session has been started, enter **www.ciasupport.co.uk** in the **Address Bar** and press <**Enter**>.

2. The home page for this site contains two hyperlinks, the word **here**, and the text **CiA Training Website**, both shown in blue. Both will open new web pages without having to enter an address. Move the cursor over the first hyperlink, the word **here**. Notice the pointer changes to a hand, to indicate the text is a hyperlink.

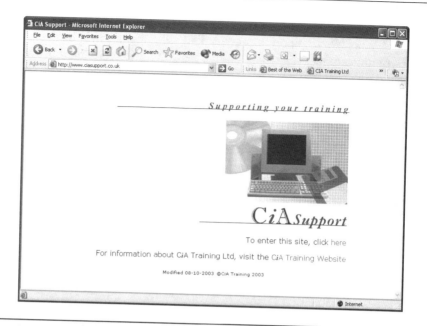

3. A **ScreenTip** is displayed with the text **Enter CiA Support** and the address of the linked page is displayed in the **Status Bar**.

4. Click with the mouse to display the contents page, as on page 77.

5. There are more hyperlinks down the left of this page. Click on the word **Hyperlinks** to move to the hyperlinks page.

6. Read the text here then click on the button that reads **An Image Hyperlink**. A new hyperlink page is displayed.

7. There is a hyperlink in the text to return to the previous page, click on it.

   ⓘ *Clicking the **Back** button would have worked just as well.*

8. The hyperlinks used so far have been to other pages in the site, scroll down the original hyperlinks page if necessary, to see a list of hyperlinks to other sites.

9. Click the link to the **CiA Training Homepage**. The **ciasupport** site is replaced by the new site.

10. Click the **Back** button to return to the **ciasupport** site.

11. It is possible to open a new linked site in its own browser window. On the **Hyperlinks** page, right click on the **BBC Online** hyperlink and select **Open in New Window**. The **BBC** site is opened, but in a new window. The existing **ciasupport** site is still open in its window. Look at the **Taskbar** to see buttons for both sites.

ⓘ *This option can be defined as the default when creating any new hyperlink.*

12. The **Back** button will not return to the **ciasupport** site because it is in a different window. Click the **Close** button in top right of the **BBC** window to close it. The **ciasupport** site is displayed again.

13. Click **Home** to return to your Home Page.

Exercise 32 - Revision: Internet Basics

1. In the browser window below, name the following parts:

e-Citizen
© CiA Training Ltd 2004

2. Which of the following statements best describes a browser?

   a) A software application that allows you to create a web site

   b) A person who spends all day surfing the web

   c) A software application that allows you to move between web sites easily ✓

   d) Someone who reads magazines without buying them

3. Which of the following are correctly composed web addresses?

   a) http://e-citizen.com

   b) http://www.disney

   c) http://www.ciatraining.co.uk ✓

   d) http://www//.inland revenue.gov.uk

4. Name the following buttons, using **ScreenTips** if necessary:

   a) Favourites

   b) Home

   c) Refresh

   d) back

*Answers are listed in the **Answers Section** at the end of the guide.*

Chapter 5 - E-mail Basics

In this chapter you will learn how to: understand e-mail principles, use Outlook Express, use the Inbox, create and send a message, open a message, reply to and forward a message, send and open attachments, use address books. To do the exercises in this section you will need an active e-mail address. These are usually provided as part of the package when arranging Internet access through most ISPs. If not, you can get a free e-mail address from Hotmail, Virgin, Tiscali, Freeserve or AOL, for example (at time of writing).

E-mail Principles

E-mail (or electronic mail) is the transmission of messages and information electronically, usually between computers connected via the Internet or any internal network.

Today e-mail is an extremely important business tool and many businesses would almost come to a standstill without it. It has obvious advantages over the normal postal system: mail is delivered within seconds rather than days. Rather than pay excessive postage for sending paper copies of files through the post or by courier, electronic files can be attached to e-mail messages. All the sender pays is the cost of a local telephone call, or probably a lot less if they have a broadband connection. Consider how much more quickly business documents can be sent overseas using e-mail than by using normal post or airmail.

ISPs and e-mail accounts

Usually the **Internet Service Provider** (**ISP**) who provides Internet access will also supply one or more e-mail accounts and addresses. These are areas in their computers that are reserved for your e-mails. When you send an e-mail from your computer, it goes to this area and is transmitted into the Internet. Incoming mail addressed to you is stored in this area until you connect to it and download the messages to your computer.

It is possible to set up an e-mail account that is web based, rather than an account linked to a specific computer, so that messages can be collected and sent by an individual, from any computer with an Internet connection.

Before using e-mail, familiarise yourself with the rules of netiquette - network etiquette. Always use accurate and brief subjects in the appropriate field on a message. Keep your messages brief and relevant rather than rambling. Make sure your outgoing messages are spelled correctly.

Junk mail (spam)

Be prepared to receive unwanted e-mails. As they are so easy to send, certain companies and individuals send out masses of junk e-mails (often known as **spam**), just like the unwanted postal mail you receive. Unfortunately, junk e-mail is not always harmless - some of it can contain inappropriate or offensive material. Some ISPs automatically filter incoming mail to remove junk e-mail before it reaches you. Although some may occasionally get through, you are shown later in the guide how to delete unwanted messages.

Viruses

Unfortunately, e-mails today are one of the main routes for viruses to enter your computer, usually via e-mail attachments. Viruses are malicious programs written specifically to enter computer systems unnoticed and cause nuisance or harm.

Viruses are covered in a later section, but you should ensure you have up to date anti-virus software installed on your computer and treat all messages without a subject, or from an unknown source with caution. Save attached files to disk and scan them for viruses before opening if you are at all suspicious.

Exercise 33

Some of the following statements apply mainly to messages received via e-mail, some apply mainly to those received via the normal postal service, and some apply equally to both. For each statement answer **e-mail**, **normal**, or **both**.

1. They can include unsolicited junk.

2. You need a computer to read them.

3. They can include pictures of your dog.

4. The dog can eat them.

5. The cost of sending does not depend on how far they are going or how much content there is.

6. They can include physical objects.

7. They need an address.

> *Answers are listed in the **Answers Section** at the end of the guide*

Using Outlook Express

There are many software applications available for messaging, which all follow the same basic principles. *Outlook Express* is installed with *Internet Explorer* and is a simplified version of the messaging system used in the separate application, *Microsoft Outlook*.

> *Users of Outlook 2000, XP, 2003, Hotmail or Yahoo Mail can download instructions for this e-mail section at **www.learnersworld.co.uk**. Click the **Added Extras** drop down list and choose the appropriate software from beneath **How to Use**. The password required to open the document is **ciamail** (note that passwords are case sensitive).*

Outlook Express manages all electronic messages coming to and going from the computer. Messages can easily be composed and sent to any e-mail address; files can easily be added to a message. If *Outlook Express* is not running, messages are stored in your account for you until they are collected.

E-mail addresses

A valid e-mail address is needed before you can send or receive mail. An address, e.g. **charlie_brewster@somewhere.co.uk** cannot contain spaces and consists of:

a **user name**	*charlie_brewster* the name of the mailbox where the server forwards incoming mail. It must be unique within the domain name
an **@** sign	separates the user name from the domain name
a **domain name**	*somewhere.co.uk* the address of the computer which sends and receives e-mail

Exercise 34

1. To start *Outlook Express*, select **Start | All Programs** (Programs *in Windows 2000*) | **Outlook Express**.

    Alternatively, Windows XP should always include an icon in the Start Menu to start your e-mail application.

    Outlook Express must be configured before it can be used for the first time. Configuring is simply the term used to describe the supply of user information to the server, who manages the mail. For home users connecting through a commercial ISP, Outlook Express will normally be configured as part of the installation procedure. Once the required information has been supplied, e-mail can be used.

    For networked computers, if the Internet Connection Wizard starts, contact your IT Administrator, who will be able to configure Outlook Express.

2. If there is no Internet connection active, *Outlook Express* will display a dialog box informing you that you are working offline and ask if you want to connect or continue working offline. Choose to connect.

3. If your setup requires it, the **Dial-up Connection** dialog box will appear allowing logon information for a specified user to be added. Enter the required information and the *Outlook Express* screen will be displayed after a few seconds.

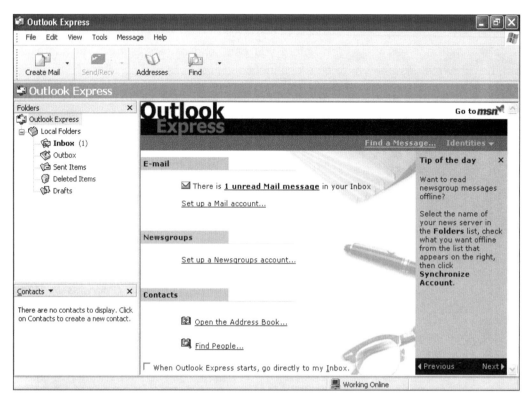

> (i) *If the first screen shown is the **Inbox** screen instead of the one above, the next two steps are unnecessary. Move to step **6**.*

4. At the bottom of the screen is a check box: **When Outlook Express starts, go directly to my Inbox**. Ensure this box is checked (this will ensure the **Inbox** is always shown first, which saves time when next opening the application).

5. A list of available folders is shown in a pane on the left. Click on the **Inbox** name from this list to open the **Inbox** folder.

6. Leave this screen open for the next exercise.

The Inbox

Outlook Express has a **Folders List** at the left of the screen, e.g. **Inbox**, **Sent Items**, etc.

The **Inbox** is where details of all incoming messages are displayed and where these messages can be processed (searched, read, deleted, etc.). It is possible to change the **Inbox** screen **View**, e.g. whether to preview messages before opening or not.

Exercise 35

1. The **Inbox** screen should be open from the previous exercise.

    It may be that there are no received messages here yet. If this is the case it might be useful to visit this exercise again at a later time, when there are messages present.

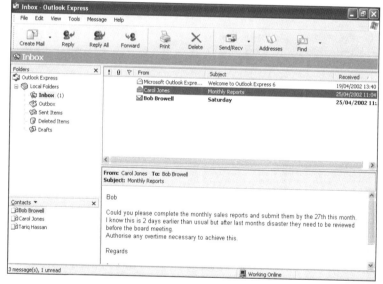

2. The top pane at the right of the screen lists all messages in the **Inbox**. Messages in bold type have not been read yet. Those messages which are not bold have been read. Notice the icons to the left of the messages, ⬜ or ⬜.

    To delete a message, click on it in the top pane and then press <Delete>.

3. Click on the other folder icons, then select the **Inbox** again.

4. Select **View | Current View** to see the available options. Select **Hide Read Messages** to list only unread messages.

5. Select **View | Current View | Show All Messages** to make sure that all messages, read and unread, are shown in the **Inbox**.

6. Select **View | Layout** to display the **Window Layout Properties** dialog box. The screen display can be changed from here.

7. The top part of the screen controls which components are displayed. Removing the check from a component will remove it from the display.

8. Normally, the contents of messages in the **Inbox** are previewed in their own pane at the bottom right of the screen. To hide this **Preview Pane**, remove the check from **Show preview pane** in the **Preview Pane** area.

9. Click **OK** to apply the new settings.

10. Select **View | Layout** and replace the **Preview Pane** in the correct position, then click **OK**.

*Some viruses can be activated by previewing incoming messages, so on your own computer it may be advisable to leave the **Preview Pane** switched off.*

e-Citizen
© CiA Training Ltd 2004

Creating a Message

Outlook Express allows messages to be easily created using many features found in word processing applications.

Exercise 36

1. From any *Outlook Express* display, select the command **Message | New Message**. The **New Message** window is displayed.

    ⓘ *The **Create Mail** button,* [Create Mail ▾]*, can also be used to display the **New Message** window.*

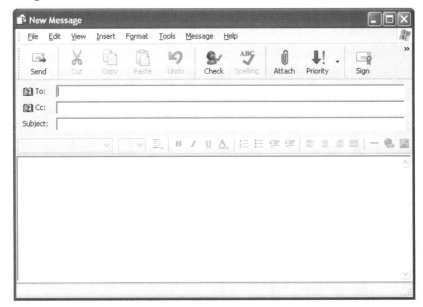

2. The window looks similar to a word processing application with a few extra lines beneath the first toolbar. The **To:** box will contain the address for the message. Type your own e-mail address here (so the results of this exercise can be observed).

    ⓘ *Clicking the **To** button,* [📖 To:]*, will display any addresses listed in your **Address Book** (see Exercise 41). These can then easily be inserted into the **To** box. Addresses can be added to the **Cc** box to send copies of the message to these people.*

3. In the **Subject** box, enter **Test message**.

4. Type in the following text in the main part of the window: **Always remember to check your e-mail regularly!**

5. Double click on the word **regularly** to select it, then press <**Delete**>.

6. Insert the new text, **at regular intervals throughout the day**.

7. Select all of the text and use **Format | Font** to change its **Font**, **Size**, and **Color**. Click **OK** when complete.

8. Position the cursor at the beginning of the text and click the **Spelling** button, 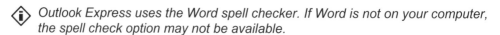 to spell check the message.

    Outlook Express uses the Word spell checker. If Word is not on your computer, the spell check option may not be available.

9. Examine all the menus from **File** to **Help** in the **Test message** window to see what options are available. Note that there is a **Save as** option so that the message could be saved and modified later before sending.

10. Leave the **Test message** window open for the next exercise.

Sending a Message

You can send an e-mail message to anyone, as long as their address is known.

Exercise 37

1. With the new message created in the previous exercise still open, click the **Send** button, .

    *The command **File | Send Message** or the key press <**Alt S**> can be used instead.*

2. The **New Message** window is closed and the message is transferred to the **Outbox** folder.

3.   Click **Outbox** in the **Folders** list to see all messages waiting to be transmitted, including the **Test message** that has just been sent. *Outlook Express* can be configured to transmit all messages immediately, in which case the message will already have been moved to the **Sent Items** folder.

4.   If the **Outbox** still shows the message, click [Send/Recv]. When this button is clicked, *Outlook Express* also downloads any incoming mail.

5.   When the message has been sent, click on the **Sent Items** folder. A copy of each sent message is kept here, so you can see the **Test message**.

6.   It can sometimes take a few minutes for messages to be received, so move to the next exercise to make sure your self addressed message has arrived.

Receiving a Message

Messages are received in the **Inbox**. Once a message has been read, its icon will change to an opened envelope, ✉.

Exercise 38

1.   Open the **Inbox** folder in *Outlook Express* and click the **Send and Receive All** button, [Send/Recv]. A dialog box will appear temporarily to say that *Outlook Express* is checking for new messages.

2.   Watch the new messages appear in the **Inbox** message pane. There should be at least one message (the one sent to yourself in the previous exercise). Notice that the **Subject** text, **Test message**, is included in the **Inbox** entry. Consistent use of **Subject** text will make messages much easier to sort and identify.

   *If the message has not arrived, wait for a few minutes and try **Send and Receive** again.*

3.   To read a message, either click on it once, then view its contents by scrolling down the preview pane, or double click to actually open it and see the whole message. Click on the **Test message** and read its contents in the preview pane.

> If the preview pane option has been switched off, the only way to read a
> message is to double click on it to open it.

4.   Notice how the envelope icon is now open and the message is no longer in bold
     type. By default, messages are marked as read after being previewed for a few
     seconds.

> This default time can be changed within **Tools | Options**, on the **Read** tab. To
> mark a message as **Unread**, select it, then select **Edit | Mark as Unread**. The
> envelope icon changes to closed and the text to bold type.

5.   Read any other messages which are present.

6.   Double click on the **Test message** to open it. It is shown in a window similar to the
     New Message window.

7.   Close the **Test message** by clicking the **Close** button, ⊠ in the top right corner of
     its window.

Reply to/Forward a Message

As well as reading incoming messages, there are options in the **Inbox** to reply to the sender,
reply to everyone to whom the message was sent, or to forward the message to new
recipients with some added text. When replying to a message, the original text can be
included or omitted.

Exercise 39

1.   Select the **Test message** from the list of messages in the **Inbox**.

2.   Click the **Reply** button, [Reply] , to display a message window, with the address of
     the sender of the original message automatically inserted in the **To:** box. The original
     message is displayed.

> The **Reply All** button is used to reply to all recipients of the original message.

3.   If you do not want the original message to appear in every reply you send, it can be
     omitted automatically. Close the reply message form and select **Tools | Options**
     from the **Inbox** menus.

4.   Click the **Send** tab.

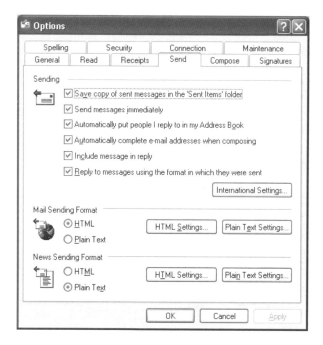

5. Remove the check from **Include message in reply** and click **OK**.

6. To see the new settings, click **Reply** again. Notice how the original message is no longer included.

7. Notice that **Re:** has been automatically inserted at the front of the **Subject** text indicating a reply to a previous message. This makes it easy to identify replies when browsing your Inbox.

8. Enter the following message text: **Thank you for your informative message. I am sure it will be of great benefit to me.**

9. Click **Send**, then **Send and Receive**.

10. To change the settings to their default status, select **Tools | Options** and the **Send** tab, then replace the check in **Include message in reply**.

11. Click **OK** to confirm the change.

Original messages can always be removed from any particular reply by highlighting the text and deleting it.

12. Select the **Test message** again, then click the **Forward** button, .

13. When the message form is displayed, click in **To** and enter a friend's address.

14. The **Subject** section begins with **Fw:** indicating a forwarded message. Extra text can be typed in the main window, to be included with the original message. In the **Subject** box, delete the text except for **Fw** then enter **Forwarding messages** after **Fw:**.

15. In the message area, enter the following text, above the original message: **This message may be of interest to you as well.**

16. Click **Send**, then **Send and Receive**. The message has been forwarded to a friend.

Attaching files to E-mails

It is possible to attach any sort of file to an e-mail message in *Outlook Express*. This makes it easy to send reports, charts, sound files or pictures, for example. Although any type of file can be sent, the recipient must have the appropriate software to be able to access it. For example if an attached database was produced in *Access XP*, the recipient must have a compatible version of *Access* to open it.

When the message reaches its destination, the paperclip icon adjacent to the envelope, 0 ⊠ , will let the recipient know there is an attachment.

The attachment can be opened, and/or saved for reference.

Exercise 40

1. Within **Inbox**, click the **Create Mail** button, .

2. Enter your own e-mail address in the **To** box and enter the **Subject** as **Attachment**.

3. In the message area, type the following text:

   Please look at the attached web page and let me know if it is of any interest to you.

4. Click the **Attach** button, ![Attach], and the **Insert Attachment** dialog box will appear.

Insert Attachment ? X

Look in: My Documents

Access 2003 Advanced Data
Access 2003 Intermediate Data
Bills work
CiA Support_files
Dawn
ECDL Ops Manual Updates

Excel 2003 Advanced Data
Excel 2003 Intermediate Data
FrontPage 2003 Introductory Data
Home test e-Citizen
My Data Sources
My eBooks

File name: [   ] Attach

Files of type: All Files (*.*) Cancel

☐ Make Shortcut to this file

5. From the **Look in** drop down list, select the location where your files are stored, then click on the required file. If you have completed Exercise 14 of this guide, select the file **Training Web.htm**, which will be found in **My Documents**.

6. Click **Attach**. All attached files are listed in an **Attach** box, which opens up in the message header area just under the **Subject** box.

7. To attach a second file, repeat steps **4** to **6**, this time selecting a different file before clicking the **Attach** button.

> *If a file is attached in error, the attachment can be deleted by selecting its entry in the **Attach** box, then pressing <**Delete**>.*

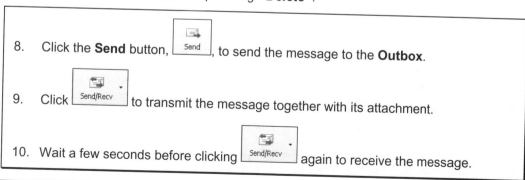

8. Click the **Send** button, [Send], to send the message to the **Outbox**.

9. Click [Send/Recv] to transmit the message together with its attachment.

10. Wait a few seconds before clicking [Send/Recv] again to receive the message.

11. Double click on the message to open it. To open the attachment, double click on the icon in the **Attach** box of the message.

12. There may be a warning dialog box displayed asking if you want to open the attachment or save it to your computer, because of the threat of viruses from e-mail attachments. If so, select the **Open** option. The appropriate software starts automatically, displaying the contents of the attached file.

13. Look at the content and then close the application that was opened.

14. With the message still open, select **File | Save Attachments**.

File | Save Attachments can be run from the main Inbox menu without opening the message. The message with the attachments must be selected.

15. When the **Save Attachments** dialog box appears, ensure **Save To** shows the location in which you wish to store the attachment, e.g. **My Documents**. An example is shown below, saving an **htm** file attachment.

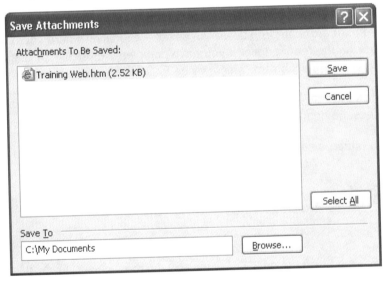

16. Click **Save** to save the selected attachments. If more than one attachment is listed, select the one required (or click **Select All**).

Because of the risk of viruses, some organisations insist on all attachments being saved to a designated area so they can be virus checked before opening.

17. Close the message but leave *Outlook Express* open.

Address Books

A very useful feature of the program is the **Address Book**, which stores information about contacts. If a contact's e-mail address is entered here, it saves the need for remembering addresses.

Once details are entered in the address book they can be used in messages without having to type them again. Address Book entries can be created automatically from incoming messages or message replies.

Exercise 41

1. Click [Addresses] to display the **Address Book** dialog box.

2. Click the **New** button, [New], then select **New Contact** from the list. The **Properties** dialog box for **Contacts** is displayed.

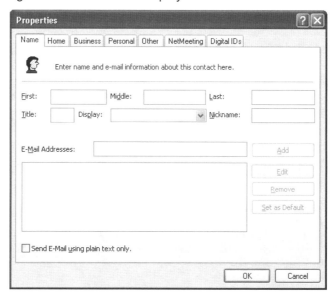

3. A large amount of data can be entered under the various tabs, creating a database of contact information, but for messaging purposes only entries under the **Name** tab are required. Enter your own details in the dialog box, clicking **Add** after entering the **E-Mail Address**.

> ⓘ *If a **Nickname** is entered, a message can be addressed to that person by typing only their nickname in the **To** box of the message.*

4.   Click **OK** to add the record.

5.   In the same way, add the names and e-mail addresses of four friends to the **Address Book**. An address book list with names added is shown.

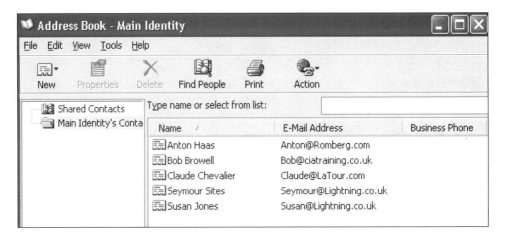

6.   Close the **Address Book** window.

7.   There is a quick way of adding details to the address book for someone who has sent you a message. Right click on a message from them in the **Inbox**. A shortcut menu is displayed.

8.   Select **Add Sender to Address Book** from the menu.

9.   Open the **Address Book** and scroll down the list to see the new entry.

> ⓘ *To automatically add senders of messages, to which replies have been sent, to the address book, select **Tools | Options | Send** and click **Automatically put people I reply to in my Address Book**, then click **OK**.*

10. Close the **Address Book**.

> ⓘ *The **Address Book** can be used to add an address when creating a message. From the message window, click the **To** button, [📖 To:]. Double click on the required name from the list and click **OK**. The address appears in the **To** box.*

11. The contact just added to the **Address Book** has decided to move to a desert island, with no forwarding address. Open the address book again.

12. Select the contact.

13. To delete this e-mail address from the list, click the **Delete** button, , on the toolbar of the **Address Book**.

14. Click **Yes** at the prompt to delete the contact's details.

15. Close the **Address Book**.

16. Close *Outlook Express*.

Exercise 42 - Revision: E-mail Basics

1. Which of the following is a valid e-mail address?

    a)   jamesbrown@ciatrain.co.uk

    b)   www.jamesbrown.com

    c)   jamesbrown#ciatrain.co.uk

    d)   James Brown@ciatrain.co.uk

2. Which of the following can be transmitted as an attachment to an e-mail?

    a)   Image file

    b)   Spreadsheet

    c)   Presentation

    d)   Any of the above

3.   What is stored in the **Outbox** of *Outlook Express*?

    a)   All transmitted messages

    b)   All messages waiting to be transmitted

    c)   All messages

    d)   All unread messages

4.   What is stored in the **Inbox** of *Outlook Express*?

    a)   All received messages

    b)   All received messages which have been read

    c)   All messages

    d)   All unread messages

5.   Which one of the following statements about the **Reply** function is <u>not</u> true?

    a)   You can send a reply to the person who sent the original message

    b)   You can send a reply to everyone who received the original message

    c)   You can send a reply to someone not mentioned in the original message

    d)   You can include the original message text with the reply

6.   Which one of the following activities is only possible when you are connected to the Internet?

    a)   Create e-mails

    b)   Read e-mails

    c)   Receive e-mails

    d)   Delete e-mails

7. You send an e-mail to someone who is not currently online. What happens to the message?

    a)   It is held on your computer until it can be sent

    b)   It is held on your ISP server until it can be sent

    c)   It is held on the recipient's mail server until it can be received

    d)   It is lost and must be re-sent

8. You receive an e-mail that may be important but you suspect it may contain a virus. What of these options the best course of action?

    a)   Open it carefully

    b)   Save it without opening and virus check it

    c)   Leave it for a few days before opening

    d)   Delete it

    ⟨î⟩ *The answers are listed in the **Answers Section** at the end of the guide.*

1

Block 1 Revision

This exercise covers all the topics introduced throughout the whole of Block 1.

Exercise 43

1. Which of the following is an Output Device?

    a) Keyboard

    b) Mouse

    c) Monitor

    d) Mouse mat

2. The term **click**, when referring to use of the mouse, has a specific meaning. Which of the following is the correct meaning?

    a) Press and release the left mouse button

    b) Press and release either the left or right mouse button

    c) Press and release the right mouse button

    d) Press and hold the left mouse button

3. Windows that are not maximised can be moved by clicking and dragging. Which part of the window should the mouse pointer be placed over to move it?

    a) The centre of the window

    b) An edge of the window

    c) The Title Bar

    d) The bottom right corner of the window

4. A dialog box may provide many different ways of choosing options or giving commands. Which of the following items will NOT be found in a dialog box?

    a) Tab

    b) Option button

    c) Restore button

    d) Check box

5. You wish to save your word processing document in a format that can be viewed on the Internet. Which of the file types below should you choose?

   a)   .doc

   b)   .html

   c)   .xls

   d)   .rtf

6. You wish to save your word processing document in a format that can be read by most word processing applications. You are not concerned about maintaining any existing formatting. Which of the file types below should you choose?

   a)   .doc

   b)   .rtf

   c)   .dot

   d)   .txt

7. When preparing to print a document, which of the following settings cannot be adjusted from within the **Print** dialog box?

   a)   The number of copies printed

   b)   The orientation of the page

   c)   The range of pages to be printed within the document

   d)   The printer to be used

8. **Folders View** can display different views of files that are contained within a selected folder. Which of the following settings will allow you to see the dates on which the files were last modified?

   a)   Thumbnails

   b)   Icons

   c)   List

   d)   Details

9. Which one of the following items is not needed to enable access to the Internet

   a)   Internet Service Provider

   b)   Modem

   c)   Speakers

   d)   Browser software

10. Which of these statements is true?

   a)   Internet and the World Wide Web are two names for the same thing.

   b)   The Internet is the collection of information stored on a vast number of connected computers.

   c)   The World Wide Web is a vast computer network.

   d)   The World Wide Web is the collection of information stored on a vast number of networked computers.

11. Open a new word-processed document and enter your name and the date as a title. Below the title, list the steps involved in adding to your **Address Book** the e-mail address of someone who has sent you a message. Save the document as **Address.doc** in **My Documents**.

12. Create a folder called **Block1** in the **My Documents** folder.

13. Move the file **Address.doc** from the **My Documents** folder to the **Block1** folder.

14. Copy the **Address.doc** file in the **Block1** folder, then rename the copied file as **Second.doc**.

15. Delete the **Block1** folder and all of its contents.

16. Start an e-mail application and open a new message form.

17. Address the message to **e-citizen@ciasupport.co.uk** and enter **Block 1 Revision** as the subject line. Type the following text into the body of the message:

   Dear CiA Support Team

   Thank you for providing such high quality training materials. I feel sure that this Open Learning Guide will enable me to become a competent e-Citizen.

   Yours sincerely

   I M Grateful

18. Send the message.

   *Answers are listed in the **Answers Section** at the end of the guide.*

Block 2

Information Search

This Block makes you aware of the nature and extent of information available on the Internet in the areas of news, government, consumer, travel, education/training, employment, health, interest groups and business.

You will be able to search for information from a wide range of Internet sources using browsing and keyword search techniques and be able to retain the information in a useful format.

You will also appreciate some of the issues and risks associated with using the Internet, such as reliability of information, secure access, viruses, unsolicited e-mail, security of personal data and parental control to access, and be able to take some precautionary measures.

Chapter 6 - Searching

In this chapter you will learn how to: use a search engine, use search criteria, search using navigation features, search for information, copy and paste text from a web page, save a web image, save and print a web page, bookmark a web page.

Searching

Navigating around the World Wide Web can be a somewhat slow and aimless process, especially for beginners. It is possible to search for specific information using the browsing techniques mentioned in Chapter 4, particularly following hyperlinks up and down through a series of sites until the relevant information can be located. This can be an erratic process.

Sites called **portal sites** have been developed to assist the navigation process. A portal site acts as a starting point for web browsing. It often contains links to many other sites categorised into headings like Jobs, Travel, Entertainment, links to current news and sports items, links to financial information such as share prices, links to online shopping facilities, and usually a general search engine facility. Portal sites are ideal as a user's home page and many ISPs provide their own portal sites for their users. The *Microsoft* site **www.MSN.com** shown in Exercise 29 is a good example of a general portal site.

Finding particular information from the vast number of sites available can be a difficult task, but it can be made easier by the use of search engines. A search engine is a site connected to a powerful database. Once you have entered key words, the search engine will select every site on its database containing those words. Some major search engines at the time of writing are:

Google	**www.google.com**
Yahoo	**www.yahoo.co.uk**
Ask Jeeves	**www.ask.co.uk**
BBCi	**www.bbc.co.uk**
Lycos	**www.lycos.co.uk**

Each search engine has a search box, where you enter details of the subject you want to find. A common problem encountered is that a search can produce hundreds of thousands of

hits (matches), not all of them relevant to the intended subject. If more than one word is entered as the subject, the default is to find sites that contain all words somewhere within the text, not necessarily together. Most search engines will sort the results so that the more relevant sites, e.g. those where the two words are together, will be shown first. It is possible to change the search by using certain criteria:

Use lowercase text	This will search for lower <u>and</u> uppercase words.
Include key words	Enter a **+** before the key word, e.g. **films +Scorcese**. This is now the default for most searches anyway.
Exclude words	Enter a **-** before an unwanted word, e.g. **french wine -champagne**.
Use phrases	In speech marks, for words which always go together, e.g. **"Tom and Jerry"** or **"The Battle of Hastings"**. Only sites that contain the whole exact phrase will be retrieved.
Specify the language	If available, use the **Language** option in the search box.

However, searching is often a case of trial and error - you must be prepared for a small degree of frustration from time to time!

> *An alternative to a search engine, a **subject directory** classifies web sites by subject. Clicking on the relevant subject will take you into progressively more detailed lists, from which a selection can be made. Directories tend to lead to fewer sites than a search engine, but they will all be much more relevant. Most search engine sites contain these directories.*

Exercise 44

1. Start your **Browser**, e.g. *Internet Explorer*, and enter **www.google.co.uk** in the **Address Bar**. Press <Enter> and the **Google** search engine is launched.

2. In the search box, enter the following search: **movie releases**. Notice how beneath the search buttons the option to search the entire web is selected.

The screen may be slightly different to the one above

3. Click on the **Google Search** button below the box.

4. After a few seconds **Google** will retrieve every site on its database which contains these words. Take note of the number of results (blue bar near the top of the results). Some commercially sponsored sites may be displayed at the top of the list or on the right side of the screen. Select the first web site match and browse the site.

5. Click the **Back** button, [Back], until you reach **Google's** home page.

6. Now, to narrow the search, from the options select **pages from the UK**.

7. Click **Google Search**. Note the number of results, which should have reduced.

8. Go back to the **Google** home page and delete the existing search keywords.

9. You want information about holidays in Australia. In the search box, type **holiday australia**.

10. Ensure the <u>entire</u> web is to be searched and start the search. A large number of matches will be found.

11. To refine the search to specifically find cheap holidays, add the word **budget** in the search box after the others to find sites containing all three words (in some search engines a **+** criterion is needed before any word that must appear on the page).

12. Start the search. There should now be fewer matches.

e-Citizen
© CiA Training Ltd 2004

13. Select a site from the list by clicking on its hyperlink. Read the information on the home page, then return to the **Google** home page by clicking the [🔙 Back ▾] button.

14. To see another example of narrowing a search, try to find web sites about sea angling. Start by searching for **angling**. Note the number of matches, i.e. the number of pages containing the word **angling**. There should be many thousands.

15. Now search for pages containing the two words **sea angling**. The two words can be anywhere on the page. There may still be several thousand but the number should be less than before.

16. Next search for the phrase **"sea angling"**. Use speech marks around the phrase. Now the words must occur together. The number of matches will be further reduced.

17. Often search engines and navigation will be combined in a search. Having used a search engine to find a site relevant to your query, navigation links (text hyperlinks or image links) from the original site can then be clicked on to find the particular information that you are seeking. Change the search criteria to **"sea angling" ireland** and search again.

18. Assume you are trying to arrange a sea angling holiday on the south coast of Ireland. Click on any of the listed sites and then click on the image links or hyperlinks it contains to find details of locations that offer such holidays.

19. Try to find details of actual accommodation. You may have to try more than one site to find the information you require.

20. Write down the full address of the page that contains the information.

*Internet Explorer includes the **Autosearch** function - a quicker, simple to use way of retrieving matches. It is possible to find the web site of a large multinational company, **Esso**, for example, by entering their name in the **Address Bar**, then pressing <**Enter**>.*

21. Click the **Home** button, [🏠], to return to your default Home Page.

Bookmarks

After browsing the web, it is likely that you will have visited some sites that you would like to revisit on a regular basis. *Internet Explorer's* **Favorites** feature provides a quick way of doing this. In a few steps your favourite sites can be added to a list which, when clicked, will take you directly to that site. This is known as **bookmarking** a web page.

Once a list of bookmarks has been created, it can be displayed by clicking the **Favorites** button. Any site from the list can then be visited by a click of the mouse. The **Favorites** list is not deleted at the end of a session. Entries stay on the list until specifically removed.

Exercise 45

1. Click on the drop down arrow of the **Address Bar** and select the **Disney** home page from the list (or type **www.disney.go.com** in the **Address Bar**).

2. Browse the site, then use the **Back** button to return to the **Disney** home page.

3. When the **Disney** home page is displayed, click ⟨☆ Favorites⟩ to display the list of current favourites in the **Favorites Bar**. The contents of the list will vary depending on which pages have already been added.

4. To add a bookmark, click the **Add** button, ⟨Add...⟩. The **Add Favorite** dialog box is displayed.

> ⓘ Alternatively, selecting the command **Favorites | Add to Favorites** from the **Menu Bar** will display the dialog box without having the **Favourites Bar** open.

5. Edit the text in the **Name** field to just **Disney Online**.

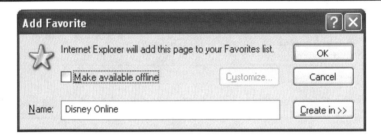

e-Citizen
© CiA Training Ltd 2004

6. Click **OK** to add the **Disney** page to your list of favourites.

7. Click on the **Home** button, [icon], then enter the address **www.ciasupport.co.uk** in the **Address Bar** and press **<Enter>**.

8. Browse the site, then use the [Back] button to return to the site home page.

9. When the **ciasupport** home page appears, repeat steps **4** and **6** to add it to your list of favourites, use the name **CiA**.

10. Click on the **Home** button, [icon], then enter **www.nasa.gov** in the **Address Bar**. Press **<Enter>**.

11. Browse the **NASA** site, then return to its home page using the [Back] button.

12. When the **NASA** home page is displayed, repeat steps **4** and **6** to add it to your list of favourites, use the name **NASA**.

13. Return to your default **Home Page** by clicking [icon]. Several sites have now been added to your favourites.

14. To display a bookmarked site, select **Disney Online** from the entries listed in the **Favorites Bar** to go directly to that site.

15. Return immediately to your default Home Page using the [Back] button and if required, close the **Favorites Bar** by clicking its **Close** button, ⊠.

Saving a Web Page

Having found the information you require on the Internet, there is often a need to transfer some of that data to your own computer.

Entire web pages can be saved directly from the Internet so that they can be viewed later without an Internet connection. They are saved in the same way as other files or folders, either on the hard drive or floppy drive of the computer, using the **Save As** function within the browser. Individual items from a web page, e.g. images, sounds, or other specified objects can also be saved. As an alternative to saving, some web page items, e.g. URL, individual images, blocks of text, may be transferred directly into other applications, using standard **Copy** and **Paste** functions.

There are copyright implications when using any items obtained from the Internet. Basically any image, audio, video, text file, program or other item on the Internet is protected by internationally recognised copyright legislation, unless specifically identified by the owner as copyright free and available for general use. You should not use or distribute any material from the Internet unless you are sure that copyright issues do not apply.

Exercise 46

1. Create a folder named **Information** within **My Documents**. This can be used to store evidence of what you have found in this Block.

2. Create a word processing document with a name of **Pages Visited** and save it in your new **Information** folder. Make sure the document is open.

---

3. Use any method to go to **www.ciasupport.co.uk** web site and move through the site to the **Downloads** page.

4. Click once in the **Address** field to highlight the URL for this page.

---

5. Select **Edit | Copy**. Use the **Taskbar** to switch to the **Pages Visited** document, then either click the **Paste** button, ⧉, or select **Edit | Paste**. The address is inserted into the document.

6. Press **<Enter>**. The address is automatically formatted as a hyperlink to the **Ciasupport** site, http://www.ciasupport.co.uk/Downloads.htm .

7. Switch back to the browser window and click and drag to highlight the first paragraph of text on the page.

Downloads

This page contains downloads - two sound files, one video file and a software program. To download and view these files without saving, simply click the file and follow the instructions described in your Open Learning guide. To download and save a file to a created folder, right click on the file and follow the instructions described in your Open Learning guide.

8. Select **Edit | Copy**.

9. Use the **Taskbar** to switch to the **Pages Visited** document, then either click the **Paste** button or select **Edit | Paste**. The text is inserted in the document.

> http://www.ciasupport.co.uk/Downloads.htm
>
> This page contains downloads - two sound files, one video file and a software program. To download and view these files without saving, simply click the file and follow the instructions described in your Open Learning guide. To download and save a file to a created folder, right click on the file and follow the instructions described in your Open Learning guide.

10. Use any necessary formatting to enhance the appearance of this document.

11. Switch back to the browser window. To save the whole page, select **File | Save As** from the menu. The **Save Web Page** dialog box will appear.

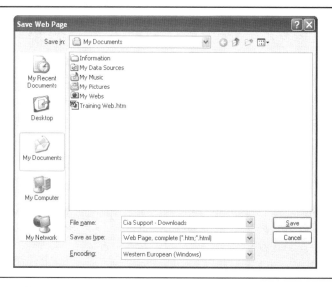

12. In the **Save in** box, specify the location where the file is to be saved, in this case double click on the **Information** folder.

13. Make sure **Save as type** shows **Web Page, complete**.

14. Change the **File name** to **Sample** by overtyping the existing name and click **Save**.

15. Right click on the hyperlink text **Berlioz.wav** and select **Save Target As** from the shortcut menu. A **Download** message box may appear briefly.

16. In the **Save As** dialog box, select **Information** as the saving location and make sure **Save as type** shows **Wave Sound**. Click **Save**.

17. Click the **Images** link on the left of the screen to go to that page.

18. Right click on the image of the CD. Select **Copy** from the shortcut menu.

19. Switch to the **Pages Visited** document, and paste the image onto a new line in the document.

20. Alternatively the image may be saved as a separate file. Switch back to the browser, right click on the CD image and select **Save Picture As**, near the top of the shortcut menu shown above.

21. In the **Save Picture** dialog box, change the file name to **Testimage** and select **Information** as the saving location. Leave the type as **JPEG (.jpg)**.

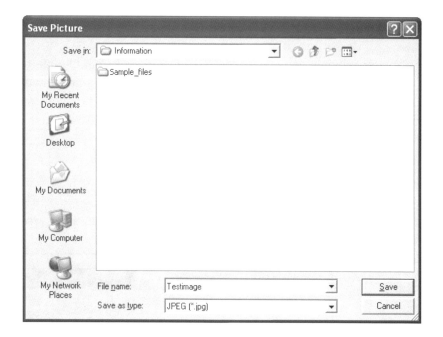

22. Click **Save**.

23. Minimise *Internet Explorer* and *Word*, then open **My Documents** from the **Desktop**. **Sample.htm**, **Berlioz.wav** and **Testimage.jpg** should all be in the **Information** folder.

24. Double click **Sample.htm** and it will be displayed in its own *Internet Explorer* window. The page can be displayed at any time, without the need for an Internet connection, i.e. offline, because it is now downloaded on to your computer.

25. Close the new *Internet Explorer* window and double click on **Berlioz.wav**. The sound will play (check that the speakers are on), again offline. Close your media player.

26. Double click on the **Testimage** file. The image will be opened in whatever application is set as your default image viewer. Close the image and the application.

27. Delete all the downloaded files and close **My Documents**.

28. The **Pages Visited** document will be used again throughout the guide. You can either leave it open now, or close it then open it again when required.

29. Maximise the original *Internet Explorer* window.

Printing a Web Page

Internet Explorer can print pages, or parts of pages, directly from the Internet. The user can decide which parts of the web page to print. If the page is **framed** (made up of different areas), individual frames or selected frames can be printed, or the page can be printed as it appears on the screen. It is also possible to print all documents linked to the web page, or a table of links. A page can be previewed before printing.

Exercise 47

1. With the **Ciasupport Downloads** page on screen, select **File | Print** to display the **Print** dialog box.

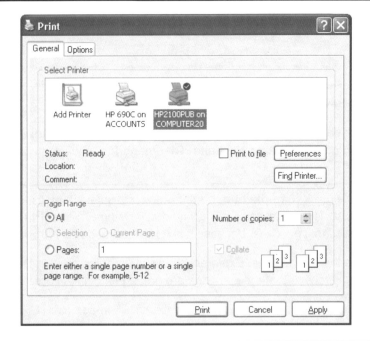

2. Select the appropriate printer and in the **Page Range** section, select to print page **1** only, and make sure that **Number of copies** is set to **1**.

*The **Selection** option is ghosted unless part of the page has already been highlighted.*

3. Under the **Options** tab, make sure that the check boxes **Print all linked documents** and **Print table of links** are either unchecked (not ticked) or ghosted. Opt to print the frames **As laid out on screen** from the **Print frames** section.

4. Click **Print**.

 The **Print** button, can be used to print a single copy of the page on the default printer using default settings without displaying the **Print** dialog box.

5. Click the **Product Support** link from the links bar on this screen. When the page is displayed, click and drag across the bulleted list in the main panel to highlight it in blue.

6. To print only the selected text, select **File | Print**. From **Page Range** choose **Selection** and click **Print**.

7. Click the **Home** button, .

Exercise 48 - Revision: Searching

2

1. Which of the following is a well known search engine?

a) Sniffer

b) Dongle

c) Google ✓

d) Dougal

2. Which of the following search criteria should find the least number of sites?

a) peanut

b) peanut butter

c) +peanut +butter

d) "peanut butter"

 correct

3. Which of the following is made easier by using a search engine?

    a) Connection to the Internet

    b) Finding relevant sites *correct*

    c) Downloading files

    d) Browsing the World Wide Web

4. Which of the following applies to an image saved from the Internet?

    a) It cannot be deleted unless the Internet connection is active (online)

    b) It can be viewed when the Internet connection is inactive (offline) *correct*

    c) It will be automatically updated as the image on the Internet is changed

    d) All of the above

5. Which one of the following statements about **Favorites** sites is true?

    a) Any **Favorites** sites can be opened offline

    b) Any site can be added to the **Favorites** list *correct*

    c) Sites cannot be deleted from the **Favorites** list

    d) A deleted site will be automatically removed from the **Favorites** list

6. Which one of the following statements about printing web pages is true?

    a) Pages can be printed directly from the Internet *correct*

    b) Prints of pages can never include graphics

    c) Only whole pages can be printed

    d) Pages must be downloaded before printing

> The answers are listed in the **Answers Section** at the end of the guide.

Chapter 7 - Precautions

In this chapter you will learn how to: understand computer viruses, use virus protection software, understand the need for firewalls, recognise the risks of inappropriate web content, apply content restrictions, understand the general risks of Internet access.

Computer Viruses

A computer **virus** is a piece of malicious software code introduced to a computer system, with the ability to spread itself to other computers. The extent of the harm caused by viruses varies enormously. Some can lie dormant until triggered by a particular date or time and then merely cause annoyance, by displaying unwanted messages, for example. Some cause real damage, by deleting data from the system or by seriously disrupting the computer's operation, for example; others attempt to identify sensitive information within a computer and transmit it to another location using e-mail or an Internet connection.

New viruses appear daily and introducing any information to the computer from an external source that is not 100% trusted is a potential source of virus infection. Today, by far the most common method of virus transmission is via e-mails. It is relatively easy to control what software you load on to your own computer, but it is not so easy to control who sends you e-mails. Even opening an e-mail message to read it can introduce a virus and some viruses, as part of their effect, copy themselves and transmit themselves to e-mail locations they find in the computer's address book.

The problem is so widespread that some experts have predicted that it will cause the end of e-mail as a communication method. Whilst this may be an exaggeration, it is perhaps a measure of the severity of the problem.

Exercise 49

Are the following statements true or false?

1. Computer viruses are mainly transmitted via e-mails. *T*

2. If your computer is running OK you do not have a virus. *F*

3. All viruses will cause you to lose all your data. *F*

4. Viruses can spread between networked computers. *T*

5. Computer viruses can be spread to family pets. *F*

6. New viruses appear almost every day. *T*

7. Viruses can appear spontaneously on your computer. *F* *you must let it in*

8. You can transmit a virus to another computer without realising it. *T*

> *Answers are listed in the **Answers Section** at the end of the guide.*

Virus Protection

To combat the increasing threat of computer viruses, there are many versions of virus protection software available. Basically these operate in two modes.

Firstly, they can scan a computer system for existing viruses. These scans can be started manually or can be put on a schedule so that they run at certain times. All or part of the system can be scanned. Most protection applications also offer the option of removing viruses that are found and reversing their effects where possible. This process is known as **disinfecting**. If this is not possible, there is often the option to **quarantine** the infected code by moving it to a safe area where it will cause no further damage.

Secondly, they can run continuously to shield (auto-protect) a system from incoming viruses. Possible sources of viruses such as floppy disks and network connections are automatically checked and reported on, if necessary. Some applications extend this cover in certain circumstances by checking e-mail even before it has been processed by the computer.

Unfortunately most common virus protection programs currently have an inherent problem. They work by scanning the code in a system and comparing it to a list of all known viruses. If a match is found, a virus has been detected. So the only viruses a protection system can detect are ones it already knows about. When a new virus first appears, it must be identified and added to the list of known viruses. The user must then obtain a copy of this new list to update their system before they are protected against the new virus. It is not enough to install and run virus protection software, it must be continuously updated with the latest list.

Most protection applications can be updated by downloading the current virus list (or the new additions to it) via the Internet on a regular basis. Some systems can even transmit new additions to virus lists automatically as they become available.

Virus protection systems now exist which try to identify viruses by their actions, or to detect virus activity as it occurs. The development of anti-virus software is expected to be rapid and dramatic over the next few years.

There are many versions of virus protection software currently available from a range of suppliers. As an example this exercise looks at one, **Norton AntiVirus**, available from **Symantec**. The manual for your particular application will include specific instructions.

Exercise 50

1. Locate the virus protection application on your computer. If it is found in the **Start** menu, (**Start | All Programs | Norton AntiVirus** for example) there may be a choice of options. Select **Norton Antivirus** from the list to show the main window.

    ⓘ *If you are unable to access virus protection software, read this exercise for information only.*

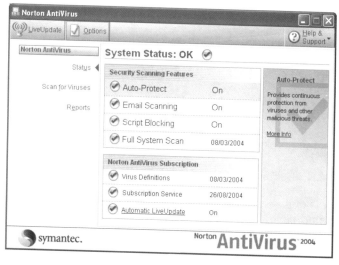

2. The default view shows the status of your system. In the previous diagram, **Auto-Protection** is activated and is set to include e-mails and scripts (a type of virus) and **Automatic LiveUpdate** of the latest virus definitions is running. The full system was last scanned on **08/03/2004**, the virus definitions were last updated on **08/03/2004**, and the updates are available until **26/08/2004** when a new subscription will be payable.

3. To set the options for anti-virus operation, click [✓ Options].

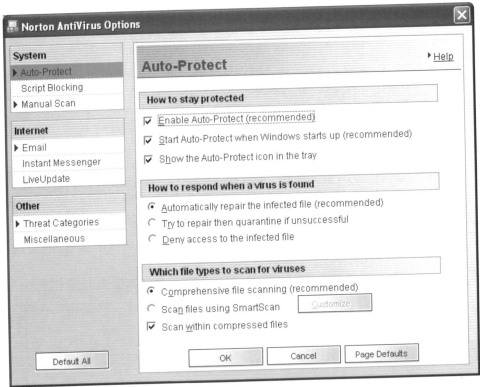

4. Look at the options available then click **Cancel** to return.

5. To start a single virus scan, select **Scan for Viruses**.

   *This option is sometimes installed as a **Desktop** icon, or as a button on the Taskbar.*

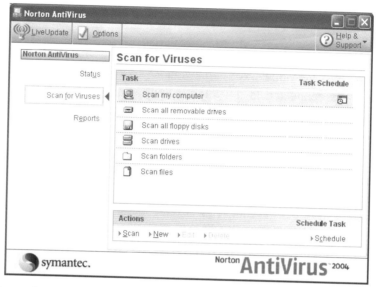

6. Examine the options to see which parts of the system can be selected for scanning, from the entire computer to individual files. Double click **Scan my computer** to scan the whole system. As the scan is running, a progress window is displayed.

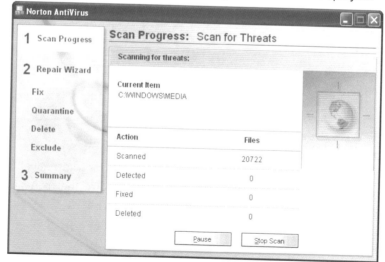

7. When the scan is completed a summary report is created showing the results, including any corrective actions which were taken.

8. Close the **Summary** window and click the **Close** button to shut down the anti-virus window.

Firewalls

Any computer that is connected to the Internet is vulnerable to the attentions of external sources. Malicious individuals and organisations routinely scan for any computers that are switched on and connected to the Internet. Any such computer is visible to these scans. Once a vulnerable computer has been identified, it is possible for the external source to access the hard drive or network drives and make use of any data stored there, or even take control of the computer.

To counteract such activity a **firewall** should be installed. The firewall is effectively a filter that determines what type of traffic is allowed to pass out of the system to the Internet, and into the system from the Internet. This usually takes the form of software running on your computer that can be configured to restrict certain external access, although sometimes the firewall can be a separate computer on a network with the sole task of connecting to the Internet. This computer is the only one that can be seen from outside and will contain no data. Other computers on the network can send and receive Internet requests from that machine. An advantage of a hardware based firewall is that if any sustained attempt to access the system is detected, the firewall hardware can be switched off or disconnected, therefore quickly and easily cutting off the system from the Internet.

Firewalls can be configured in different ways to give different types and levels of protection. It may be set to allow only e-mails to enter the system or alternatively, to block incoming traffic from specific sources known to be malicious. To give the highest level of security, a firewall can be set to prevent any unauthorised incoming traffic, while allowing traffic to pass outwards. The computer will effectively operate in stealth mode, appearing invisible to any external scans, as if it were not connected to the Internet.

A disadvantage of firewalls is that they can also question external connections to your computer by legitimate applications, for example downloads of software upgrades, music and video samples. If access is configured as optional, an excessive number of prompts can be generated, asking if each access attempt is to be allowed.

Exercise 51

Fill in the missing words in the text, using the appropriate word from the list below:

software, Internet, configured, traffic, firewall, protection, filters.

Any computer connected to the (**a**) is vulnerable to attack. A (**b**) can be installed to help prevent this. The firewall (**c**) the traffic between your computer and the Internet. It normally takes the form of (**d**) running on your computer. Firewalls can be (**e**) in different ways to give different levels of (**f**). The firewall can be set to prevent unauthorised incoming (**g**), but to allow (**g**) to pass outward.

*Answers are listed in the **Answers Section** at the end of the guide.*

Parental Control

There is an unbelievable amount of data on the world wide web. There are sites representing every aspect of human life. It follows then, that there may be content on the web which is offensive to even the most broad-minded person. Indeed, there is some content placed on the web for the sole purpose of being offensive.

Whilst the average person may consider the occasional inadvertent view of offensive material an acceptable price to pay for unrestricted access to the web, there are situations where all possible steps should be taken to prevent this, particularly in the case of access by children. At the time of writing there are no restrictions of any kind built into the Internet, anyone can access anything. There are, however, external methods of imposing control. Internet browsers (and some firewalls) include content filters, which can allow or restrict access based on a rating system or by individual site. Commercial software is available which will restrict access to sites based on content and by individual site. This software often includes the ability to monitor and restrict chat room access, currently an increasing area of concern.

Exercise 52

1.   Select **Start | Control Panel**.

2.   Open **Internet Options**.

   *If you are in **Category** view select the **Network and Internet Connections** category first.*

3. Select the **Content** tab of the **Internet Properties** dialog box and look at the buttons in the **Content Advisor** area.

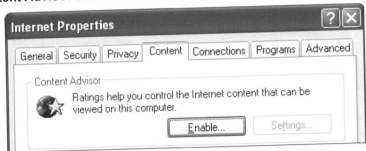

> If **Content Advisor** is currently enabled, there will be a **Disable** button rather than an **Enable** button. If **Content Advisor** has never been activated, the **Settings** button will be unavailable.

4. To change the **Content Advisor** settings when it has not yet been activated, click **Enable**. If it has been activated, click **Settings**, enter the Supervisor password if prompted and click **OK**.

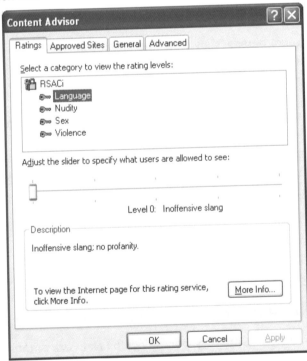

5. Click on each **Category** and set the slider to the required level of access.

6. Click the **Approved Sites** tab and enter addresses (**URL**s) of specific sites that can **Always** be viewed or **Never** be viewed.

7. Click the **General** tab. There is an option to allow users to see any site that does not have a rating. If this is not selected, only sites with the required ratings can be viewed.

8. There is also a button here to allow the **Supervisor Password** to be changed (the original password must be known). Setting a password here for the first time will activate the system. The password is case sensitive.

9. Click **Cancel** to ignore any changes, including activation.

    > *Only click **OK** to accept the settings and possibly activate the system if you are sure that is what you want. Once activated, the **Content Advisor** system can only be enabled, disabled or amended by using the password. The password will always be required.*

10. Close the **Internet Properties** dialog box and the **Control Panel** window.

Data Security

When making purchases on the Internet it will usually be necessary to supply financial data (usually credit or debit card details) to the seller. This process involves some risk (although probably no more than supplying the same details over the telephone) and so there are protection methods available to make the process safer. Making online financial transactions with a bank or insurance company for example carry the same level of risk.

Many web sites cannot be accessed without a user name and password; these are called **protected** sites. Sometimes you have to pay a fee up front before you can access a web site, which can then be done by entering the user name and password allocated to you. You will usually need a user name and password to shop online at supermarkets such as Sainsbury's or Tesco, and to use online financial services.

[handwritten: Can set up for JUNK MAIL.]

Most sites that involve supplying sensitive financial data, e.g. shopping and banking sites, will be set up as **secure sites**. This means that all transferred information will be automatically encrypted (scrambled).

These web pages can be identified by **https** at the start of the **URL**, and a small padlock symbol, 🔒, on the **Status Bar**. <u>Always ensure that you are using a secure site before supplying any financial or other sensitive information.</u>

Exercise 53

[handwritten: WWW.NETWORKSECURITY GUIDE.NET]

1.   Use a search to find out what encryption involves.

2.   Why do you think encryption is used when transmitting sensitive data? *[handwritten: TO SAVE ANYONE KNOWING]*

3.   How can a secure site be recognised? *[handwritten: WITH A GOLD PAD LOCK]*

4.   What do you think could be the additional security implications of entering sensitive information such as passwords on a publicly accessible computer? *[handwritten: HACKERS]*

     ⓘ *Answers are listed in the **Answers Section** at the end of the guide.* *[handwritten: COULD MAYBE ACCESS IT]*

Other Risks

Many of the risks involved in using e-mail messaging and accessing the Internet are the same as those found in other aspects of everyday life, although they are sometimes made worse by the very power of the Internet.

Junk e-mails (also see Chapter 5)

Everyone has received unsolicited junk mail through the postal system, and the electronic mail system is no different. It is probably more widespread with e-mails because it is much easier to do. An e-mail advertisement can be sent to 10,000 addresses with a single click (once the address list has been created). In rare cases e-mails can be used with malicious intent. An organisation can be bombarded with so many of these e-mails that their systems become clogged and it becomes difficult for them to carry on their normal business.

e-Citizen
© CiA Training Ltd 2004

Normally however, it is an easier matter to scan your **Inbox** and delete all messages which look as if they are junk without even opening them. Just as it is now becoming possible to register with a system to restrict junk mail received through the post, some **ISP**s are offering similar systems to cut down on junk e-mails.

Fraudulent or Hoax e-mails

Any message, whether received via e-mail or through the door, which promises riches, prizes, or rewards in return for a cash payment or supplying your bank/credit card details should be regarded with the suspicion it deserves and be deleted or thrown away immediately. Some more subtle tricks have included official-looking e-mails supposedly from banks, etc., asking you to confirm card details and/or PIN numbers. <u>Delete them.</u> Banks will never ask for such information to be put in an e-mail. On a slightly less serious level, false messages have appeared warning you that you have a virus on your computer and you must delete certain files to remove it. When you do this you find that your computer will no longer function. <u>Be suspicious of all e-mails from unknown sources.</u> If in doubt, it is a good idea to get a second opinion. Preferably ask someone with experience of Internet/e-mail matters and whose opinion you trust.

Personal Data

Take as much care with your personal details on the Internet as you would in other areas of your life. Do not send financial details unless you are sure of the site and secure access is in force. Only e-mail such information if you are very sure you know where it is going. Always think before giving out details such as name, address and telephone number. This is particularly true in social situations such as e-mail correspondence and chat room activities. It is relatively easy to ignore someone electronically by deleting their e-mails or staying away from a chat room, but not so easy if they have your real name, address and telephone number.

Reliability of data

Information retrieved from the world wide web is as reliable or unreliable as data obtained from any other source. Always consider the source when judging reliability. For example it is reasonable to assume that information from the BBC web site will be as reliable (or otherwise) as that contained in BBC broadcasts. Information obtained from unrecognised web sites will be the equivalent of being told something by a man in the pub. An extra problem with web sites is that it can be more difficult to establish their authenticity. It is relatively easy for an individual to create a web site that looks prestigious and may even mimic the appearance of a larger organisation. The legislation, which normally prevents this, is a lot more difficult to apply to the world wide web, where sites may originate from any country in the world.

Advertisements

Similar points can be made regarding advertisements on the web. Whilst there are quite stringent regulations controlling advertising appearing in print or on TV, these are almost impossible to impose on web sites. Always try and get independent confirmation of any advertisements before acting on them.

Consumer Rights

In principle, buying online is covered by the same consumer rights as buying from a shop. There are some additional entitlements which apply to Distance Selling (this includes selling by mail order, telephone or on the Internet).

For example you are entitled to:

- clear information before you buy

- confirmation of the order after it is placed

- a cooling off period allowing cancellation and a full refund

- a full refund if goods or services are not supplied within the agreed timescales, or within 30 days

In practice, whilst reputable companies will adhere to these rules, it will be very difficult to enforce them for every site on the web, many of which will be based abroad. As a minimum safeguard, try to deal only with sites which provide a postal address and/or telephone number, although this is by no means a guarantee. Be particularly careful of online auctions, where consumer rights are even more difficult to apply.

Exercise 54

Are the following statements true or false?

1. All e-mails contain some form of virus. F

2. People contacted in chat rooms can lie about their true identity. T

3. Many commercial web sites contain advertisements. T

4. You have no consumer rights when buying online. F

5. Information on web sites is more reliable than from any other source. F.

Exercise 55 - Revision: Precautions

1. Which of the following is <u>least</u> likely to introduce a virus to your system?

    a) Opening an e-mail

    b) Sending an e-mail ✓

    c) Downloading a file from the Internet

    d) Copying a file from a floppy disk

2. No virus protection system is 100% effective. Which one of the following is the main reason for this:

    a) Viruses can appear from nowhere

    b) Viruses can be hidden in normal code

    c) No two viruses are the same

    ✓ d) Viruses are usually only detected after they have been discovered and identified

3. Which of the following can be scanned by virus protection software:

    a) Folders

    b) e-mails

    c) Floppy Disks

    d) All of the above ✓

4. The difference between firewalls and virus protection software is:

    a)   Firewalls detect viruses before they enter the computer

    b)   Firewalls control access to the computer from external sources ✓

    c)   Firewalls detect hardware malfunctions

    d)   All of the above

Prevent Hackers Getting into your Pc

5. Which of the following entries on a web site will guarantee that the content is genuine:

    a)   Guaranteed Genuine

    b)   Government Approved

    c)   British Banking Service Certificated

    d)   None of the above ✓

6. What can you communicate in a chat room with complete safety:

    a)   Your address

    b)   Your credit card number

    c)   Your opinion

    d)   All of the above

7. Which of the following is normally used to purchase something on the Internet:

    a)   Credit or debit card ✓

    b)   PIN number

    c)   Cheque book

    d)   Cash

8. Where is control of Internet content usually applied?

    a)   On the ISP server

    b)   On the telephone network

    c)   On your modem

    d)   On your computer

ⓘ *The answers are listed in the **Answers Section** at the end of the guide.*

Chapter 8 - Information

In this chapter you will learn how to: use the techniques you have learned to browse for information in the general subject areas of news, government, consumer, travel, education/training, employment, health, interest groups and business.

Introduction to Learners World

In order to provide a consistent set of web pages to illustrate some of the exercises in this guide, CiA Training have created **Learners World**. This is an interconnected set of sample web pages designed to be used in conjunction with the guide. Although these pages simulate actual sites they do not have the full functionality of actual sites. Only the actions described in the guide will be accepted, and any details submitted will not be sent anywhere.

Exercise 56

1. Start your web browser application and display the opening page of the Learners World site at address **www.learnersworld.co.uk**. If working off line from a CD, the home page is **index.htm** within the **learnersworld** folder.

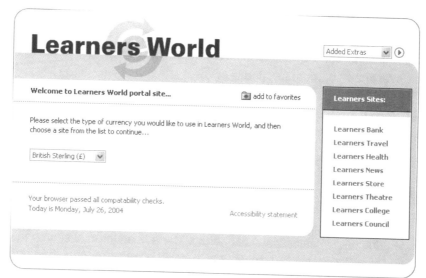

2.   Select the correct currency for your location from the drop down list. Prices will be shown in this currency on all subsequent screens. British Sterling (£) is used as the default throughout this guide.

3.   Click ![add to favourites] to bookmark this page and add it to your list of favourite sites. Click **OK** at the dialog box to accept **Learners World** as the name.

4.   Click ![Favorites] to display the **Favorites Bar**. There will be an entry for **Learners World**. Different exercises in the guide will require different sites to be opened. This entry can be clicked at any time to return to the **Learners World** home page so that a new site can be selected. Close the **Favorites Bar**.

5.   Click the **Accessibility statement** link to see the various compliance standards of the **Learners World** sites.

6.   Select **Favorites** on the **Menu Bar** and click on the **Learners World** entry to return to the site home page.

   *Clicking the **Back** button, or clicking the **return to main screen** link would also have returned to this screen.*

News

The world wide web is an ideal medium to display all kinds of up to date news stories: local, national and international. Information coming in to a central location can be quickly added to a web site which is then immediately available to people all over the world. Many television and radio stations and newspapers have their own web sites and news stories are often updated every hour, or more frequently.

Exercise 57

1.   Click the **Learners News** link on the right of the main home page to open the **Learners News** home page.

2.   Examine the various options. This is a simulated home page for a fictitious news agency showing some of the features that will be seen on actual sites. Tabs along the top frame and links in the navigation pane would lead to pages specialising in features in particular areas of interest. There is an internal search function that would find specific items and an option to set the page as your homepage so that it is always the first page shown when you start your browser.

e-Citizen
© CiA Training Ltd 2004

3. News content is shown in the central frame, including scrolling headlines about the latest stories, items about the main stories of the day, and a list of other current items. Click on the link to the full story about the holidaymakers escaping a fire.

4. Items in an actual news site will often be much longer than this and may involve using scroll bars to display the full content. For now, read this text and click the link at the bottom of the page to return to the **Learners News** homepage.

5. Use any method to go to a search engine of your choice and use the searching techniques you have learned to browse for a newspaper that is local to where you live. Use the full name to search for, e.g. Newcastle Evening Chronicle, as there may be Evening Chronicles for other towns.

6. Use the hyperlinks provided on the web site to go to a story of interest.

7. Print out the story.

8. Search for a local radio station. Use links on the site to find local news. Notice if any of the same stories as those in the local newspaper site are mentioned.

9. Now search for a national newspaper, e.g. The Times, Daily Express, or Mirror.

10. Find a top story for today and read the article. Save this web page to your **Information** folder, created in Exercise 46.

11. Search for top news stories from a national TV network, e.g. BBC or ITN.

12. Print out a story of interest.

13. Within the web site chosen, if there is a link to business news, follow it and print out a business news story.

14. Search for any large national company. Find the latest corporate news items for it.

15. Find an article of interest and save the page to your **Information** folder.

Government

Both local and national government information can be found on the World Wide Web. Most local councils have their own web site, with details of social and leisure services, information about education and public services, local political issues, statistics and much more. The government provides a large amount of information on laws and legislation, and most government departments have a dedicated web site, e.g. Department of Health, etc.

Exercise 58

1. Return to the **Learners World** home page using the **Favorites** feature and open the **Learners Council** site.

START THIS PAGE
AT ✱

2. Finding specific information, e.g. the opening times of the central multi-storey car park, may involve following a series of links. Click the **Transport** tab to display a page of links to various aspects of city transport.

3. Click the link to **Car Parks** to display a list of links to individual car park locations. In a real site, clicking the link to the required location, e.g. **Central Multi Storey**, could display a page of details including opening times.

4. For this exercise, click the link at the bottom of the page to return to the **Council** home page.

5. Search for your local council web site. If they don't have a site, search for one nearest to where you live.

6. Try to find information about the primary schools in your area. How many are there? *60 primary schools*

7. See if you can find the name of your local MP. *Mike Weir MP for Angus*

8. Find out what pest control measures are set up to help if you were unfortunate enough to have a problem, e.g. rat or cockroach infestation.

9. Save the relevant page(s) to your **Information** folder.

10. Find the most recent census statistics for your town or city. Read the information.

11. Search for services for local businesses. Is any assistance provided for new business ventures, e.g. funding or training?

✱ 12. Now go back to the home page of your chosen search engine and search on a national level for **Business Link**.

13. Find out what government assistance is provided for companies starting up.

14. If you can find guidelines for producing a business plan, print them out.

15. Now search for a copy of the Data Protection Act.

16. Copy and paste the URL of the page you have found into your **Pages Visited** document.

2

Consumer

There is a vast amount of information available on the world wide web for consumers. There are sites selling almost any item that can be sold, sites offering services such as banking and insurance, and sites covering a huge range of entertainment and cultural events.

A great deal of information can be gathered from these sites such as item specifications, comparative prices, availability, product reviews, etc. before any purchasing takes place. The use of these sites for the purchase of items or services and the booking of events is covered in **Block 3**.

Exercise 59

1. Go to the **Learners Bank** home page. This represents a simulated bank home page, showing the sort of features that would normally be available.

2. Look at the various options listed at the left of the page; these are very similar to many actual online banks. There are options to find out about the different types of available accounts, loans, mortgages and insurance, etc. Further options would exist behind the options on the first screen.

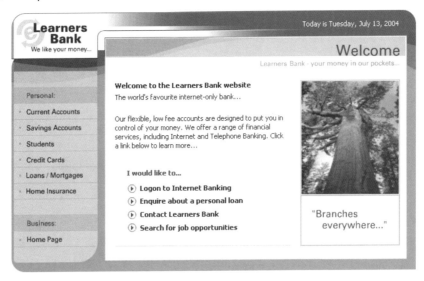

3. Click the **Current Accounts** link in the navigation pane on the left to display more information about the **Special current account**.

4. Use the **Favorites** button to return to the **Learners World** home page and then open the **Learners Store** site. This site will be used in **Block 3** to help you practise buying goods online.

5. Notice the tabs along the top of the screen, leading to different areas of the store and the navigation pane links to specific pages.

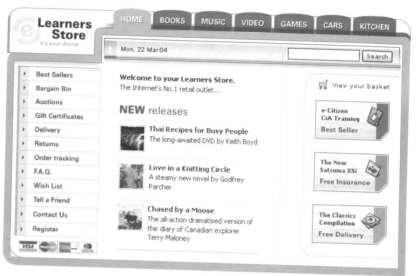

6. Click on the **Books** tab to display a list of categories. In a real site these categories could be expanded to see lists of book titles. As well as displaying goods by category, sites will usually specifically display links to items which are new or special offers.

7. Most store sites will also include search facilities so that individual items can be found. Find the **Search** text box at the top of the page; this will be used in Block 3.

8. Return to the **Learners World** home page.

9. Work through the following steps to see live banking sites and other useful consumer web sites.

10. Search for the web site of a national bank, e.g. HSBC, Barclays, and find details of a branch near to where you live.

11. Copy and paste their postal address to your **Pages Visited** document.

12. See if you can find the overdraft rate for a current account.

13. Now search for the public swimming pool nearest to where you live and see if you can find out weekend opening times.

14. Save the page to your **Information** folder.

15. Browse to find the current price for a car you would like to buy. Print the page.

16. Find a local cinema and see which movies are showing this Friday evening.

17. Choose a movie. How much does an adult ticket cost? Print the page.

18. Search for a listing of forthcoming local cultural events (exhibitions, etc.).

19. Copy and paste the URL to your **Pages Visited** document.

20. What is the next listed event and where will it take place?

21. Copy and paste the URL (if different to that in step 19) to your **Pages Visited** document.

22. Save the document.

Travel

The World Wide Web makes it really easy to plan a trip by any mode of transport. You can find timetables and shop around for prices of rail, bus and air travel, hire cars and hotels and when you've made your decisions, you can buy online. There are many sites for booking travel, accommodation, etc., separately, and many more designed to book all components of a journey in one site. The first part of any of these processes however, is to find information on such things as flight times, room availability and prices. This means that they can all be used equally well for enquiries, just remember to cancel the process before you start entering actual booking and payment details. Another point to remember is that these sites are all **live**. A hotel room that is available now may not be available an hour later when you go to book it. Alternatively there are some specialist sites which only allow enquiries, but these are usually limited to timetable information.

Exercise 60

1. Open the simulated **Learners Travel** web site to see an example of how a one-stop travel site may appear.

2. This is a typical page. Notice the links for booking flights, hotels and car hire, helpful links at the left and links to special offers in the main area.

3. Click the **Hotels** tab at the top of the page to display a simplified accommodation search page. Searching on a specific location and date range would return details of available accommodation.

4. Return to the **Learners World** home page as you are now going to look at some live sites.

5. You deserve a trip as a reward for all your hard work. In a search engine, use the search text **national rail enquiries** or **book train tickets** and find the cheapest train from Glasgow to London (you live in Glasgow, by the way) next Wednesday.

6. Check if any seats are available to match the following criteria: the train must depart around noon, but any train company can be used. The ticket is one way, for one adult.

7. Print the page showing the ticket price.

8. Check the price of a single room, with breakfast, in the Covent Garden area of London, as you have decided to stay overnight. Use a search engine with the search text of **"bed and breakfast" "covent garden"** to find some relevant sites, then navigate through some of them to find the information you want.

9. Print a page showing some relevant prices.

10. Search to see if you can find which West End shows are playing next Wednesday evening and save the page(s) to your **Information** folder.

11. While you are away from home, you fancy a short holiday abroad. Search for cheap flights from Heathrow.

12. Choose a destination and find the cost of a return ticket. Print the page showing the price.

13. You will need to see the sights while you're abroad. Find the price of a standard hire car for one week, you will collect and drop it off at the airport at your chosen destination.

14. Print the page showing the price.

15. Find the price of a single hotel room for seven nights at your chosen destination.

16. Print the page showing the price.

Education/Training

Information about education in general and specific training courses is widely available on the world wide web. Library catalogues can be searched for reference material, which can often be viewed online. Most universities, colleges and schools have web sites listing details of available courses including entrance requirements, and also league tables and other information about the establishment.

As well as the traditional courses, there are many opportunities today to participate in online courses. In these courses, students study at home or in designated centres, using information presented in specially designed web sites. All interaction with tutors, such as submitting answers or requesting advice, is done electronically. A good example of this type of **e-training/e-learning** can be found on the government's **learndirect** site.

Exercise 61

1. Open the **Learners College** web site to search for a specific course of interest.

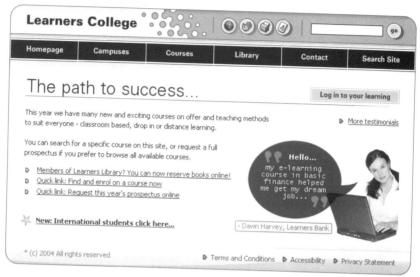

2. Click the **Courses** button. Enter **Digital Photography** in the **Subject/Course Title** box and select the **Part time** option. Click the **Go** button.

3. Only one suitable course is found. Click on its title to see more information.

4. Return to the **Learners World** home page as you are now going to look at some live sites.

5. Locate the British Library web site and navigate through the site to find the catalogue search page (the **Integrated Catalogue** at time of writing).

6. Search the catalogue for all material written by JRR Tolkien (use the author search **Tolkien J R R**).

7. Select the first match - who is the publisher? Copy and paste this information into your **Pages Visited** document.

8. Now search the catalogue for books with **sky diving** in the title.

9. How many matching items are found?

10. Go to the home page of this site and use image and text links to browse the site for information of interest to you. You may be able to read **virtual books**.

11. Search for the **learndirect** web site.

12. Find out which Spanish language courses are available.

13. Read the description of a beginner's course.

14. What is the course duration?

15. Search for a local college and find out which part time courses are available. Choose a course and search for information about enrolling on it.

16. Print out the enrolment information, or print out an enrolment form if one is available.

17. Find the **Ofsted** web site (**www.ofsted.gov.uk** at time of writing).

18. See if you can locate information about how nursery and primary schools are inspected.

19. Now try to locate a report for a specific school - perhaps one you attended as a child/teenager (**www.friendsreunited.co.uk** contains reports if you have difficulty using the **Ofsted** web site).

20. Save a copy of the report to your **Information** folder.

21. Save the **Pages Visited** document.

Employment

The government provides a lot of information for the individual or employer about employment and pension rights. On a more day to day level, it is possible to search for jobs online, to see what is available and to apply for a job that interests you, all without moving from your computer. This means that as soon as a vacancy is posted, you can apply for it without having to physically attend a job centre or similar establishment. Three main sources of job vacancy data are: government sites such as those run by the Job Centres, commercial agency sites featuring vacancies in a range of areas, and individual company sites where there is often a page specifically for vacancies and prospects within the organisation.

Exercise 62

1. Open the **Learners Bank** web site. Click the **Search for job opportunities** link on the home page.

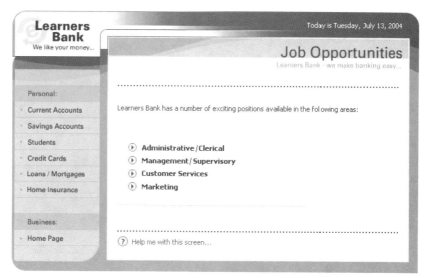

2. This is the sort of page an organisation will present to advertise its own vacancies. Click the **Customer Services** link to see a list of vacancies in this category.

3. Click the **Tellers** link to see more information on this particular vacancy. **Block 3** will deal with applying for such vacancies, but for now return to the **Learners World** home page.

4. Find a government employment site, such as **www.jobcentreplus.gov.uk** (at time of writing) and locate current news about employment.

5. Save a page containing an employment news item to your **Information** folder.

6. Use a search engine with the criteria **"employment agency"**. From the (huge) list of results, open some that cover the UK nationally and examine the types of facilities and searches that they offer.

7. Now search for a specific type of job in your area, trying any of the sites just found above, or a more general item locator site such as **www.fish4jobs.co.uk** (at time of writing).

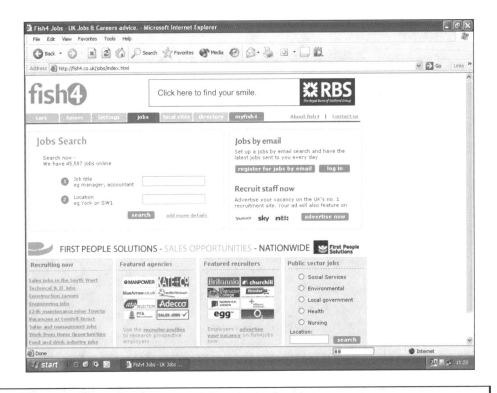

8. Print out the job details.

9. Using your chosen search engine, search for information about the **Employment Rights Act**.

10. Copy and paste the URL into your **Pages Visited** document.

11. Search for information about pension rights - try the search **Office of the Pensions Advisory Service**.

12. Copy and paste the URL into your **Pages Visited** document.

13. Now try to find information about different pension schemes, e.g. stakeholder pensions, occupational or personal pensions.

14. Save each page to your **Information** folder.

15. Save the **Pages Visited** document.

Health

Information on many health issues is available online. It ranges from information on public health, to private medicine and health insurance, to alternative medicine. There are lots of sites where you can search for specific medical conditions or complaints and perform self-diagnosis. This is not always a good idea if you have little or no medical knowledge, as you may end up wrongly diagnosing yourself with three different terminal illnesses (someone did while researching this guide)! If you <u>must</u> try to find a reason for that aching knee, visit a reputable health site such as **NHS Direct**, **Bupa**, etc.

Exercise 63

1. Open the **Learners Health** web site.

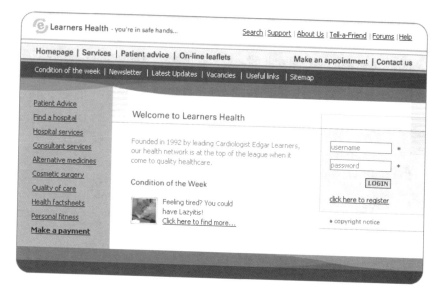

2. Study the home page to familiarise yourself with the typical layout of a site like this.

3. Notice the **login** area. Most schemes which offer interactive services will require you to register, then receive a password, to help control malicious entries. Private health schemes will often require the payment of a monthly fee.

4. The **Learners Health** site will be used again in **Block 3**, but for now return to the **Learners World** home page.

5. Locate the **NHS Direct** web site using your chosen search engine.

6. Search for information about the MMR vaccine.

7. Print a sample of the results of your search.

8. Now repeat steps 6 and 7 for asthma and tennis elbow.

9. Find out what to do if an adult has chest pain, has not had it before, but is also short of breath (answer - dial 999).

10. Now in a general search using your chosen search engine, find information about private health insurance.

11. Find out which services are offered.

12. Search for information about **homeopathy in the NHS**.

13. Copy the URL of a suitable site to your **Pages Visited** document.

14. Now search for information about herbal medicine.

15. See if you can find information about a plant that may be used to treat migraine.

16. Use a search to find out about medicines that can be bought over the counter (**over the counter medicines**).

17. Now search for medicines only available on prescription (**prescription medicines**).

18. Save the **Pages Visited** document.

Interest Groups

There are many online **discussion groups** that can be joined. These cater for all interests, hobbies, etc. and allow people to post messages about subjects that interest them. On a more serious level, many organisations such as councils will host discussion groups on their sites so that people can make comment and raise issues concerning local services. Hopefully these will be promptly answered by staff from the organisation. As replies and further messages are posted, **message threads** are created. You normally have to register with a group before posting a message.

If you prefer to meet people face to face rather than electronically, the world wide web is a good source of information about local community and special interest groups and voluntary organisations.

Exercise 64

1. Browse for information on community groups in your area.

2. At the time of writing **www.communigate.co.uk** is a useful site. It contains information on voluntary, community, special interest, religious groups, etc. for specific regions.

3. If you visit this site, look at each link to see which clubs and societies are available in your area.

4. Print any pages that interest you.

5. Use your chosen search engine to find discussion groups relating to a topic of personal interest. For example, at the time of writing, **Google's** home page has a **Groups** tab, that allows access to lists of discussion groups, or allows you to search for one.

(i) *Most search engines provide a similar service.*

6. Use the links provided in an area that interests you to find messages posted.

7. Read some messages, but do not attempt to post any yourself at this stage (see Block 3).

Business

Many companies, particularly the larger corporations, use web sites to present their organisations to the world. Most large companies will have an extensive web site giving information about their operations and although these may all look different, they usually contain the same elements. There will usually be pages containing background (corporate) information; financial (investor) information; product information; career information, and increasingly these days, environmental (social responsibility) information.

Internal computer systems are invaluable for business networking. Companies often have an Intranet system, which is an internal network of computers. This works in a similar way to the world wide web, in that it can be browsed from any connected computer, specific Intranet addresses can be entered to find a particular page, and e-mail messages may be sent across it.

Some organisations also use extranets, which provide external access to the Intranet, via an Internet connection. A company Intranet may contain such items as information about the company, human resources information, the facility to print off company documents, complete online forms, e.g. to claim expenses, overtime, etc.

Exercise 65

1. Go to the home page of the **Learners Bank** web site and click the **Business Home Page** link at the bottom left of the screen. This simulated site represents an area of a main banking web site that has been specifically designed to present links to business information about the bank itself. Information aimed at business customers is also available.

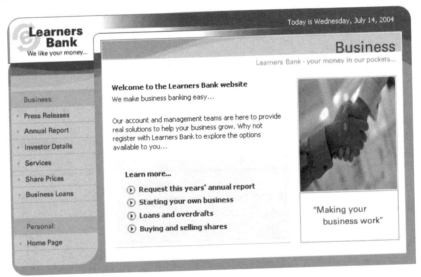

2. Study the links at the left to see the sort of information and services that would typically be available.

3. More links are available in the main part of the page, in red. Read these links.

4. Locate the web sites for some large business corporations. At the time of writing, some useful examples are **Rolls-Royce.com**, **Corusgroup.com**, **Centrica.co.uk**, **Kingfisher.co.uk**.

5. On the home page for each site, check the contents tabs to see which headings are common across all sites.

6. Browse the various sites. Notice that the content of the different pages is often held in various formats, e.g. web page, pdf document, presentation. Make a list of all the different formats encountered.

7. Try to find examples of:

   Financial results for the previous year

   Current share prices

   An organisation chart or company structure

   A list of products or product areas

   A list of employment opportunities

   Statement of policy on **Environment** or **Recycling**

8. Save a copy of each page showing examples of these features in your **Information** folder.

2

Exercise 66 - Revision: Information

1. Open the **Learners News** site. What are alternative names for:

   a) The **National**, **World**, etc. buttons along the top of the screen?   TABS ✓

   b) The area on the left with headings for a range of topics?   NAVIGATION BAR

   c) The line **Giant crab threatens bathers** in the lower part of the screen?   HYPERLINK

2. What is the destination of this week's special offer from **Learners Travel**?

   ✓ Australia (2weeks)

Block 2 Information Search

3. How many **Grand Circle** seats are left for the February 20th performance of Western Hamster Stomping at **Learners Theatre**?

    2 grand circles ✓

4. For which product is **Learnersville** world famous?

    widget making

5. On which of the **Learners World** sites would you find links to:

    a) Hospital Services?   *Health* ✓
    b) Road Works?   *Council* ✓
    c) Home Insurance?   *Bank* ✓

6. In the real world, in what alternative types of sites could you expect to find links to:

    a) Hospital Services?   *NHS* ✓
    b) Road Works?   *Council or AA, Radio*
    c) Home Insurance? →   *Insurance companies eg TSB, Prin*

Block 2 Revision

This exercise covers all the topics introduced throughout the whole of Block 2.

Exercise 67

1. Which of the following is the best defence against viruses affecting your computer?

    a) Running regularly updated anti-virus software   ✓ *right*
    b) Installing a firewall   *prevents hackers*
    c) Earthing the computer case
    d) Not using floppy disks

e-Citizen
© CiA Training Ltd 2004

2. Which of the following statements most accurately applies to Internet access on a system with no content filtering?

    a)   It is impossible to find offensive content on free sites

    b)   It is very difficult to find offensive content even if you look for it

    c)   It is relatively easy to find offensive content if you look for it ✓

    d)   You will not be able to avoid offensive content even without looking for it ✗

3. What is the effect of putting quotation marks around search criteria, e.g. "english channel" when finding sites using a search engine?

    a)   Either word must be present in the site

    b)   Both words must be present in the site

    c)   Neither word can be present

    d)   The exact phrase must be present in the site ✓ *correct*

WATERGATE — WASHINGTON — President NIXON

4. What criteria would you enter to search on **Watergate** without showing any sites referencing either **Washington** or **President Nixon**? ~~Search Engine~~

5. Use a search engine to find the answer to the following questions and include the search criteria that you used to make the search as efficient as possible

    a)   On construction machinery, what do the initials **JCB** stand for? *" JBC"*

    b)   What is the state capital of **Nebraska**? *LINCOLN*

    c)   What is the full name and date of birth of ex US president **Jimmy Carter**? *JAMES EARL CARTER 1/10/24*

6. Use a search engine to find out who founded Gordonstoun public school. Research further and find out who was the first member of the royal family to attend the school. *KURT HAHN*

7. What is the interest rate offered by **Learners Bank** on their special current account? *0·50%*

8. Go to the **Learners News** site and find out the name of the family who escaped the fire in their gîte (holiday home). *SINGH FAMILY FROM LEARNERSVILLE*

9. Copy the **URL** of the web page containing this story to your **Pages Visited** document. *DONE THAT*

URL = WEB ADDRESS

10. Copy the first paragraph of text from the story into the same document.

11. You wish to speak to someone in person to discuss obtaining a bus pass. Go to the **Learners Council** site and find out the address of the **Transport Information Centre**. *22, Muldew Street*

12. In the same site, go to the page that lists the locations of car parks in the city and find the location and capacity of the **Riverside** car park. *West of Green Park, —250 places*

13. Save a copy of the whole web page that contains this information as an **htm** file called **Parking** in the **Information** folder.

14. Go to the **Learners Store** site and open the **Cars** page.

15. Copy the mileage figures for each of the three cars and paste them in your **Pages Visited** document. *BMW = 7534*

   ⓘ Answers are listed in the **Answers Section** at the end of the guide.

Mitsubishi = 30,000

Toyota Avensis = 356

Block 3

e-Participation

The e-Participation Block launches you fully into the online world. Building on the computer and search skills already acquired, this Block completes the skills set necessary for you to become an e-Citizen.

You will be able to confidently carry out everyday tasks such as buying a CD or book, paying a bill, banking online or making a holiday reservation. You will also be able to access a variety of information services and carry out tasks such as filling in a tax return, finding out about new legislation, submitting a job application, enrolling on a course, making a doctor's appointment or taking part in an online discussion forum.

You will further appreciate some of the issues and risks associated with using the Internet, such as security risks in credit card transactions, unscrupulous online service providers and the importance of data checking in online forms, and be able to take some precautionary measures.

Chapter 9 - Online Services

In this chapter you will learn how to: complete online forms, understanding that there are various ways of entering information and become more aware of security issues.

Online Forms

Forms are web pages that will accept entered data, which can then be sent (submitted) to a specified location. There are millions of online forms on the world wide web, but the vast majority of them contain the same elements. This means that, once you have completed two or three, you should be able to complete most forms you may come across.

Exercise 68

1. From the **Learners World** home page, click the **Added Extras** drop down list and select **Online Forms**, then click the link to the **Feedback/Evaluation Form**.

2. The asterisks indicate fields that must be completed. Enter your (or a fictitious) name in the **Name** box and press <Tab> to move to the **E-mail** box. Enter a valid e-mail address. These form elements are called **text boxes**.

3. The box containing the text **Choose a Performance** is a **drop down field**. Complete this field by clicking the arrow to see a list of options, and selecting one from the list. This type of field ensures that only specific values can be entered.

4. Move down to the elements beneath the two **How would you rate...** questions. These are **option buttons** (or **radio buttons**). Select one for each question. Only one choice can be made from each selection.

5. Select answers for the next two questions from the drop down lists.

6. The boxes listing play titles, at the bottom of the form, beneath the question **Which other plays have you seen at the theatre?** are **check boxes**. Any number of these boxes can be checked if appropriate.

Which other plays have you seen at the theatre?

☐ A Midsummer's Night Dream   ☐ King Lear
☐ Macbeth   ☐ Othello
☐ Richard III   ☐ Romeo & Juliet
☐ Taming of the Shrew   ☐ Twelfth Night
☐ Hamlet

7. There are two buttons at the bottom of the form. **Submit Form** sends off the information you have entered and **Reset Form** clears all the information from the form. Click **Submit Form**.

8. An error message will be displayed. The **Date** field was defined as mandatory and has not been completed. Click **OK**, complete the date field, and click **Submit** again.

9. Correct any other reported errors until a confirmation message is shown to indicate the form has been successfully completed.

Always check all of the data on a form before submitting, as it may not be checked at the receiving end. This is essential when using a form to register for a service or to purchase items. You may not be happy to receive 12 crates of bananas from your online supermarket when you thought you were only ordering 12 bananas.

Online Security

The **Learners World** web sites provide a safe practice environment, where you can order goods and services using fake bank/credit card details. None of your personal information is retained or stored anywhere. Be aware though, that during this Block, when you move from this simulated environment to the Internet, you must always consider the security of information you submit to any web site.

Just as unscrupulous people in the real world may try to swindle customers, individuals like this also prey on Internet consumers. Always be careful about who you are providing with personal information, such as your address, bank details or credit card number, etc. A web site gives a certain degree of anonymity to the provider who creates it; just because a site looks good does not mean it is authentic. Only buy products from trusted suppliers and ensure that the padlock icon, 🔒, indicating a secure server is present before completing payment details. Be as careful in completing an online form as you would in completing paper documentation.

If you have any doubt about the authenticity of a web site, there are additional measures that can be taken to ensure it is genuine. Try only to use online service providers who supply a telephone number and postal address. You may also wish to search for information on the provider from an independent consumer research company, or from one that provides a register of legitimate companies. At the time of writing, it is possible to search for a company on the web site **www.yell.com**, where telephone numbers, addresses and web site details are supplied.   *DROP DOWN*

TEXT BOXES
OPTION BUTTONS
NAME
EMAIL ADDRESS

Exercise 69 - Revision: Online Services

1. List four elements that you might see on an online form.

2. Which button will remove all the information you have entered on a form?   *RESET FORM* ~~CANCEL~~

3. If a web site looks authentic you can safely enter information. True or false?   *F.*

4. Which symbol indicates a "secure server"?   *GOLDEN PADLOCK...*

Chapter 10 - Participation

In this chapter you will learn how to: use simulated web sites to give you the skills to perform real live tasks on the Internet in the areas of news, government, consumer, travel, education/training, employment, health, interest groups and business.

News

Although the main purpose of visiting news sites is to search for information, it is often possible to interact with such sites, for example by e-mailing your view to a local news station, participating in a news poll, or completing a form requesting your opinion of a topical news item.

Exercise 70

1. Go to the **Learners News** home page and click the link to the full **Wind turbines** story.

2. Read the story. At the bottom of the item is a link to take part in a poll on the subject. Click the link.

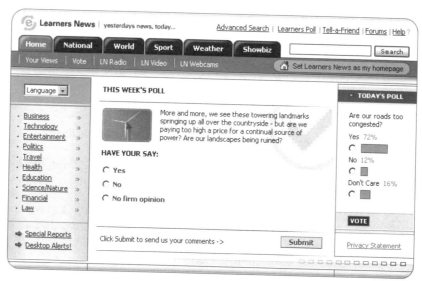

3

3. Select the **No** option and click **Submit** to send your response.

4. The next page is a confirmation that your vote has been registered, including an analysis of all the responses received so far, shown as percentages. Click the link to return to the **Homepage**.

5. As well as selecting options in a poll, it is often possible to submit your comments on a particular subject. On the home page, click the link to the item entitled **Hot Topic: Gridlock - are our roads in crisis?**

6. Read the article. There is a poll on the subject in the pane on the right, but there is also a link at the bottom of the item to **send us your comments**. Click on this link.

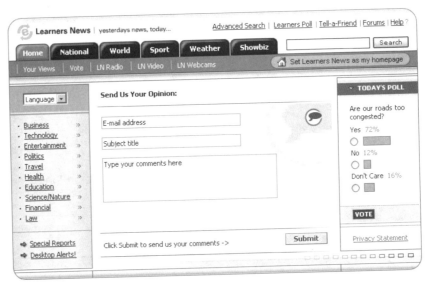

7. Type in your e-mail address (for possible replies) and a subject title.

8. Type a relevant comment in the box provided and click **Submit**.

9. The next page is a confirmation that the message has been sent. Click the link to return to the **Homepage**.

> *Some Internet links to contact or e-mail a site will result in a new message window appearing, e.g. Microsoft Outlook, with the appropriate e-mail address already entered in the **To** box. Enter your comment in the message area and then send the e-mail in the usual manner.*

10. Locate web sites for an international news agency, e.g. **www.CNN.com**, a national newspaper, e.g. **www.timesonline.co.uk** and a local newspaper, e.g. **www.sunderlandecho.com**.

11. If you can find a **Contact us** facility on these sites, list the actual site addresses used and whether each one uses forms or e-mail messaging as its contacting method in your **Pages Visited** document.

12. Complete one of the forms (or messages) with your comments on a particular subject.

13. Print out a copy of the completed form or message and submit it.

14. Find in these sites (or others) examples of items that allow you to express your views in a poll. *BBC.CO.UK*

15. Find and participate in three such polls. List each of the questions involved and your response. *MORI POLLS CHANNEL 4*

BBC Weather MITO- Price/Location Cost of a passport 35.1 64.81 Tax on holiday makers 36% Home Ownership

Government - Services

Local government web sites contain lots of information about their services and facilities for people living in the area. Some of this information is provided as informative text on the web pages, but often it is possible to download the information as a file direct to your computer. There is also usually a facility to contact the council via e-mail for specific information not provided on the web site.

Exercise 71

1. Go to the **Learners Council** web site. You are a citizen of **Learnersville** who has held a party over the weekend, which included a bank holiday Monday. As a result, your bin is very full and needs emptying, but because of the holiday you aren't sure when the refuse collection will be.

2. Click the **Contact us** button at the top right of the page.

3. Select **Refuse Collection** from the drop down list.

3

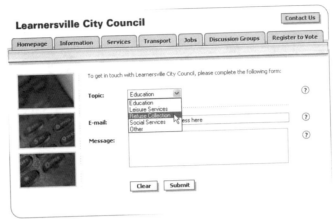

4.   Enter your e-mail address in the box provided and a message in the text box, e.g. **Please let me know when my bins will be emptied this week. I live at....**.

5.   Click **Submit** to e-mail the request for information.

6.   Click where indicated to return to the homepage.

7.   While putting more rubbish into your bin, you have been horrified to discover a nest of rats! Perhaps the council may be able to help. Click the **Information** tab at the top of the page.

8.   Information is available on a variety of topics and each item can be downloaded as either an *Adobe Acrobat* file (**pdf** format) or a text file (**rtf** format). Click the **rtf** link for **Pest control**. Click **Save** at the first prompt screen, select **My Documents** as the save location, then when prompted select to **Open** the document.

> *Security settings on some PCs may result in no **Open** prompt being displayed. If this happens, you will need to navigate to **My Documents** and open the file from there.*

9.   The pest control information is downloaded and appears in another window. Scroll down to read the information about **Rodents**.

10.   Close the document and the application used to read it, e.g. *Word*.

> *A lot of downloads are now in **pdf** format, which need the Adobe Acrobat viewer to display them. If you have such a viewer you can use the **pdf** download link. There is often an option to download the viewer program if you don't have it.*

11.   Select the **Homepage** tab.

e-Citizen
© CiA Training Ltd 2004

12. Locate your local council web site. _WWW. ANGUS. GOV. UK_

13. Try to find and download information about services they provide, e.g. travel information - bus timetables, roadwork information. _3 INFO_

14. Why not send an e-mail to the council asking for information about recycling facilities in your area?

Government - Submitting Information

Government web sites can provide a way of avoiding submitting information in paper format. This can speed up the process of completing various application forms, which at one time would all have been sent backward and forward using the postal system. Completing forms online is even quicker than taking them to the government office by hand (especially if the office is in London and you live in Derby). The Inland Revenue encourages taxpayers to complete their annual tax return online.

Exercise 72

1. Go to the **Learners Council** homepage. You have recently moved to Learnersville and want to ensure you can cast your vote in the imminent local elections. Your neighbour thinks you may be able to register online.

2. Select the **Register to Vote** tab.

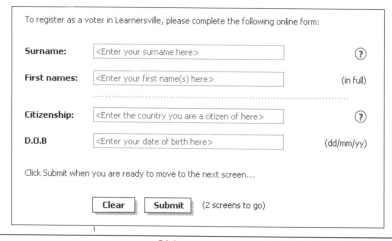

3. Complete the required information using the default entries as a guide. Click **Submit** to move on.

4. Complete the information boxes on this screen and click **Submit** again.

5. Read and check each of the boxes on this screen and click **Submit** again. A message is displayed confirming your registration.

6. Click where indicated to return to the homepage.

7. Go to **www.inlandrevenue.gov.uk** - the web site for the Inland Revenue (at time of writing all links are as stated below). Amongst other services, this site allows you to complete a self assessment tax return online.

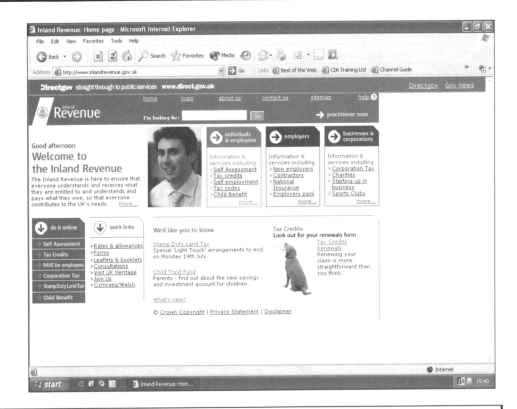

8. Click the link to **Self Assessment**.

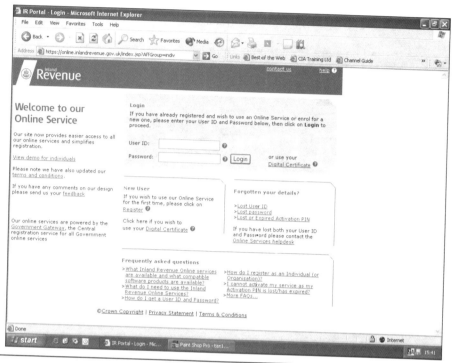

9. Read the information on screen. Before using this online service you need to be registered. If you are registered already, then you can (if you wish) complete a self-assessment form. Should you wish to register for the service, follow the instructions on screen. You will be sent an activation code, a user ID and password by post, which then allows you to log on.

10. The actual process consists of completing many pages of online forms; each entry is saved as you move from page to page. Once complete, the tax return can be submitted to the Inland Revenue.

Consumer - Banking

This exercise uses a simulated banking web site to guide you through the process of enquiring about online banking. You are then given information enabling you to log on and transfer funds between your fictional accounts. This practice will give you the skills to try it for real. In reality, you will not be allowed to use online banking unless you have already received the necessary security account numbers and passwords from your bank.

3

Exercise 73

1. Go to the **Learners Bank** home page.

2. Click the **Contact Learners Bank** link. From the drop down list, select **Online Banking Services**.

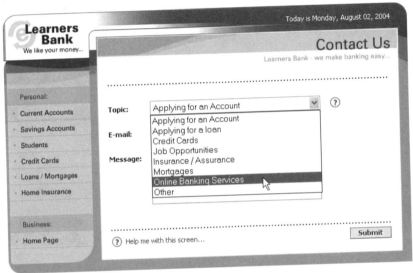

3. Enter your e-mail address in the box provided.

4. Type the following message:

> **I am a customer of Learners Bank and would like to bank online, can you help?**

5. Click **Submit**. When the **Thank you** message appears, click where indicated to return to the home page.

6. In reality, you would then receive information, usually through the post, enabling you to access your accounts online. For now, assume you already have the necessary security IDs and passwords to use online banking.

7. Follow the next steps.

8. Click the ⊙ **Logon to Internet Banking** link on the **Learners Bank** home page.

e-Citizen
© CiA Training Ltd 2004

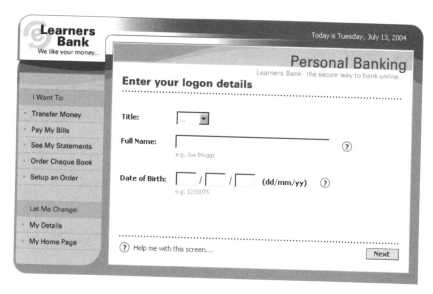

9. Choose your title from the drop down list and type your name into the **Full Name** box. Enter your date of birth in the appropriate box. Dates entered in **Learners World** sites must include leading zeros, e.g. **01/09/04**. Click **Next**.

Enter your logon details

Banking ID: [*KLB-250827*] (?)
e.g. OB123456A

Enter 7th, 9th and 11th numbers of your passcode

Passcode: [*345*] (?)
e.g. 543

(?) Help me with this screen...   Next

10. Click the **Help** button, (?), at the right of **Banking ID** to display information about this field. Read the information and then click where indicated to close the window.

11. Enter your **Banking ID OB555663B** and the required passcode numbers **567** in the boxes provided and click **Next**.

12. Your accounts at the bank are displayed. Your current account is quite healthy! Click the **Transfer money** link, ⟨ Transfer Money ⟩, at the left of the screen.

Personal Banking
Learners Bank - the secure way to bank online...

Transfer money
....

Please enter the account you wish to transfer money from:

From: Current Account : A/C 12345678 ⌄   (?)

Amount (£):   [＿＿＿＿]   (?)

On: [＿] / [＿] / [＿]   (dd/mm/yy)   (?)

....

(?) Help me with this screen...   ⟨ Next ⟩   ⟨ Cancel ⟩

13. Ensure the account you wish to transfer money **From** is shown as your **Current Account**.

14. Enter the amount of the transfer as **1500**.

> (i) *Remember that the currency is set in the **Learners World** home page.*

15. Enter today's date as the transfer date and click **Next**.

16. The account number for the transfer is **24689753** and the sort code is **98 76 54**. Enter these details now and click **Next**.

17. When the confirmation screen appears click **Transfer**.

Transfer complete
....

Please print and retain this screen for your records

Transfered: £1500

From: Current Account : A/C 12345678

To: Deposit Account : A/C 24689753

On: 14/07/04

18. At the bottom of the screen, click the link **Click here to return to your accounts**.

19. Notice the account balances have changed to reflect the transfer. Click `Log out ⊗` at the left of the screen.

---

20. If you are not currently registered for online banking, search for your bank's web site. See if you can obtain information from the bank about how to set up this facility.

21. If you don't have a bank account, search for the web site of a well known high street branch and try to find out how to open an account with them.

22. If you already have online banking set up, check the status of your accounts.

23. Don't forget to log off properly when you have finished.

Consumer - Shopping

Many different types of goods and services can be bought online. The process often follows a similar pattern: you either browse through categories or perform a specific search if you are sure of the exact item required.

Many sites offer the option to make multiple purchases. As each item is selected, it is added to an electronic shopping basket or trolley. When you are ready you can review your purchases, maybe remove, or edit some if required, then complete the purchase by entering shipping and payment details.

Exercise 74

1. Go to the **Learners Store** home page and locate the search box.

2. In the text box, type **e-Citizen** and click **Search** to search the site for any relevant books. Search facilities will often be more sophisticated than this, allowing searches to be made by different criteria, author for example.

3

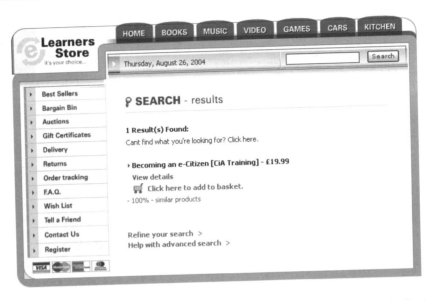

3. Only one relevant book is found and you decide to buy it. Click where indicated to add it to your basket and the screen below is displayed.

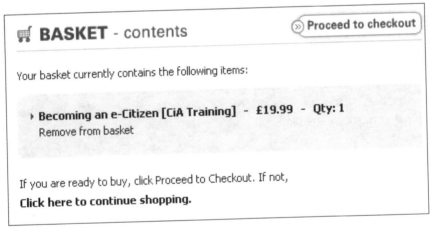

4. Select **Click here to continue shopping**.

5. Click the **Books** tab at the top of the screen to see the categories available.

6. Select the **Fiction** category to see this week's recommended fiction books.

7. Click on the title of **Shivering Sights** to see more detailed information about the book.

8. Select the **Add to Basket** link beneath the price to add it to your basket, which now contains the two books you have selected.

9. Select **Click here to continue shopping**.

10. Now select the **Music** tab at the top of the screen.

11. From the categories listed, select **Easy Listening**. This week's recommended CDs are listed.

12. Select **Sounds of the Rainforest** and at the next screen, add it to your basket.

13. Ensure the 3 chosen items are in your basket. Click [» Proceed to checkout] to go to the checkout, where the goods can be paid for.

14. The first screen allows you to review the items in your basket. At this stage, items could be removed by clicking on **Delete** beneath them, but do not make any changes.

15. Click **Next**. Enter your delivery details in the boxes provided (remember, if you wish you can enter your own details here as this is a simulated site).

16. Click **Next** again.

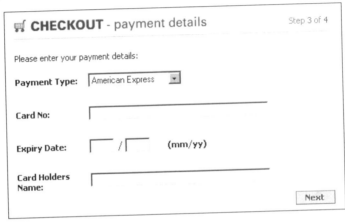

17. You are going to pay by Visa. Select **Visa/Electron/Delta** in the **Payment Type** drop down list.

18. Enter your **Card No** as **1234567887654321** and the **Expiry Date** as **04/10**.

19. Enter your name as the cardholder and click **Next**.

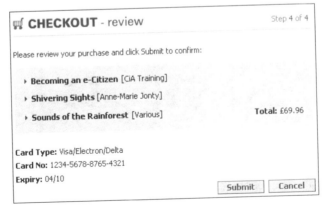

e-Citizen
© CiA Training Ltd 2004

20. Click **Submit** to confirm the order.

21. Print the confirmation page, then click where indicated to return to the home page.

Consumer - Booking Tickets

Tickets for the theatre, the cinema, music concerts and other cultural events can often be purchased online. One advantage of buying in this way is that you avoid having to stand in long queues. This exercise uses the example of booking theatre tickets.

Exercise 75

1. Go to the **Learners Theatre** web site. You have heard about a new show, featuring singing and dancing hamsters, starting in February.

2. Select the **Feb** tab. The forthcoming shows are displayed.

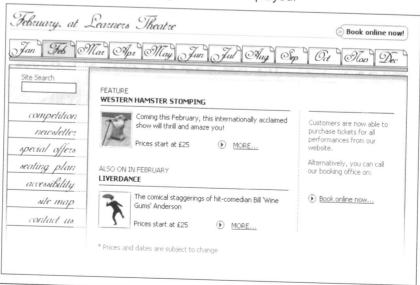

3. Click **MORE...** next to **Western Hamster Stomping** to reveal further information.

4. Select **Book online now**. Use the drop down field for the date to select the performance on **February 20** and click **Continue with booking**.

5. Select **1** ticket for the **Front Stalls**.

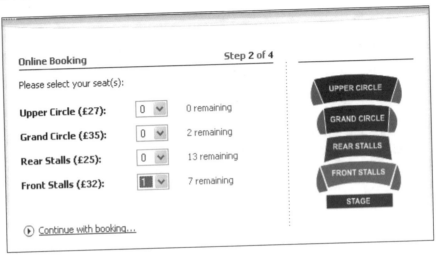

6. Click **Continue with booking...** again.

7. You will pay by **Switch/Maestro/Solo**, card number **1234567890987654**, which expires **05/10** and has an issue number of **1**. Enter your own name as **Name on card**.

8. Complete all these details and click **Continue with booking**.

9. At the confirmation page, you realise you have forgotten to check your diary and may have a prior booking for 20th. To cancel the booking, click **Cancel**.

   There will always be an option to cancel, which you may need to use, on real web sites. These steps are to show you an example of the process involved.

10. After checking your diary, you discover the 20th is free after all. Repeat steps **3** to **8**.

11. At the confirmation page select **Confirm booking**.

12. Print the confirmation and then click **Return to homepage**.

Consumer - Paying Bills

Paying bills online can save a lot of time. If you have an online bank account, you will be able to pay a wide variety of bills after logging on to your account. If not, many organisations such as local councils allow you to make online payments via credit or debit card for services such as Council Tax, for example.

Exercise 76

1. You decide you had better pay a small amount off your credit card balance. Go to the home page of the **Learners Bank**.

2. Click ⊙ **Logon to Internet Banking** .

3. Perform the log in steps described in Exercise 73 - steps **9** and **11** only.

4. When your accounts page is displayed, click ⎡ Pay My Bills ⎤ at the left of the screen.

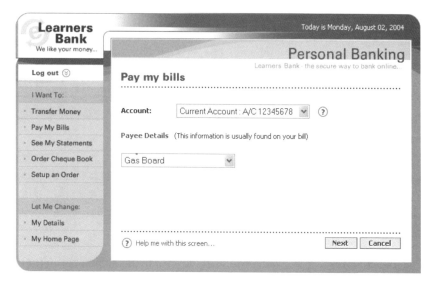

5. Make sure the account shown is **Current Account** and from the **Payee Details** drop down list select **Learners Bank Credit Card**.

3

6. Click **Next**. At the confirmation screen click **Next** again.

7. Enter the **Reference 7777-654321** and the amount as **99.98**.

8. Enter today's date and click **Next**.

9. Check the details on the confirmation screen and then click **Transfer**.

10. Click the link **Click here to return to your accounts** and then click **Log out** ⊗.

---

11. Now you are ready to make an online purchase for real. When you feel the need to buy a book or CD, for example, visit a store such as **www.amazon.co.uk** (at time of writing).

12. Follow the instructions on screen to make your purchase.

13. Try searching for a local theatre and perhaps book tickets for a show.

14. You will find, as you buy various goods and services, that most sites use a similar approach and the skills you have learned in the previous few exercises will help you through the process.

15. There is a list of useful web sites at the back of the book that you may wish to browse.

Travel

The world wide web is an ideal environment in which to book travel, accommodation and extras, enabling you to create a holiday, tailor made to your requirements. Overheads are cheaper than a high street travel agent's, therefore you can often take advantage of savings on your booking.

It is possible to book travel with organisations such as airlines and rail companies, and accommodation directly with hotels, etc. but many sites now offer the option to book all the details for a journey or holiday in one place.

Most package holiday companies also allow bookings from their brochures to be made directly on the web.

Exercise 77

1. Your task is to book a short holiday to Paris, including return flights, hotel and car hire. Open the **Learners Travel** web site and select the **Flights** tab at the top of the screen.

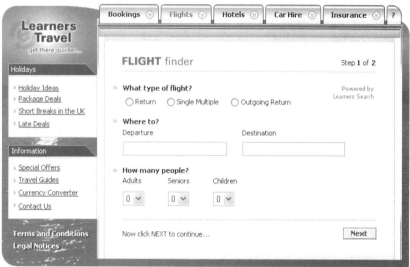

2. Complete the following information in step 1 of the **Flight finder**: **Type of flight - Return**, **Departure - London**, **Destination - Paris**, **People - 1 adult**.

3. Click **Next**. At step 2 of the **Flight finder**, enter the date you are leaving as 5th April (this year or next, whichever is first) and the date of return as 7th April.

4. You have no preference for airlines, but you want to fly economy class. Select this from the **Service Class** drop down list. Click **Search** to find suitable flights.

5.   The top set of flights are at more suitable times for you. Click **Book Now** next to the top flights.

6.   Your chosen flight details are displayed. You also need travel insurance. Select the **Single trip** insurance (£20 in Sterling) and click **Next**.

7.   Enter your own details in the **Passenger information details** boxes and click **Next**.

8.   On the **Payment details** screen select **Visa/Electron/Delta** from the **Payment Type** drop down list.

9.   Enter your **Card No** as **1234567887654321** and the **Expiry Date** as **04/10**.

10. Enter your name in the **Card holder's name** box and click **Next**.

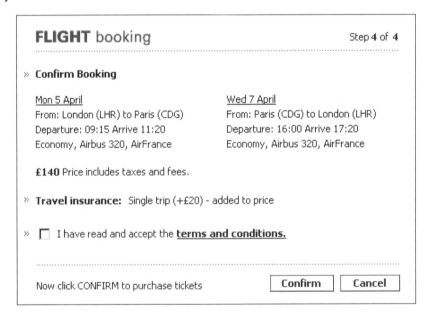

11. Confirm that all details are correct and click in the box provided to indicate that you **have read and accept the terms and conditions**.

12. Click **Confirm** to display the booking confirmation.

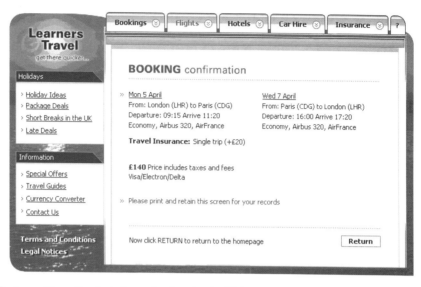

13. Click **Return**. Now the hotel can be booked. Click the **Hotels** tab.

14. You want to stay in **Paris** from 5th April to 7th April, you need **1 room** for **1 adult**. Complete the information and click **Search**.

15. On the next screen click **Book Now** to book the **Le Tour Faltay**. The available rooms are listed.

16. Book the **Standard Double**. Review your booking details before clicking **Next**.

17. Enter your own details as those of the **Primary occupant** and click **Next**.

18. On the payment screen, use the same information as entered in steps 8-10 and click **Next**.

19. On the next screen, click the **rules and restrictions** box and click **Confirm** to display your booking confirmation.

20. Click **Return** to go back to the home page. The last step is to book a hire car. Select the **Car Hire** tab.

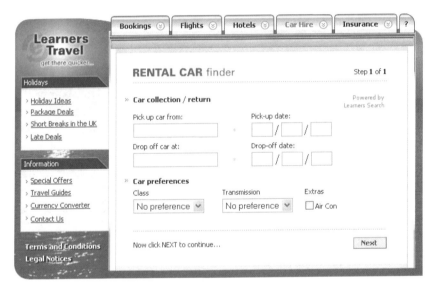

21. Use the following information to complete the screen: you want to collect the car from **Paris Airport** on **5ᵗʰ April** and drop it off at the same place on **7ᵗʰ April**. You would prefer an **Economy** car with **Manual** transmission and **air conditioning** as extra.

22. Click **Next** and choose to book the **Avis** car.

23. Review the rental details and click **Next**, then enter your details on the **Hirer information details** screen.

24. Click **Next** and enter the same payment information as in steps 8-10. Click **Next** again.

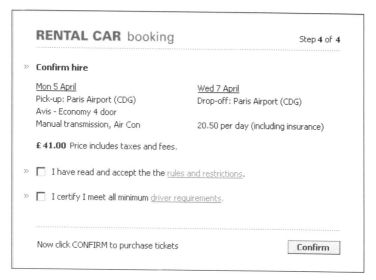

RENTAL CAR booking   Step 4 of 4

» **Confirm hire**

Mon 5 April   Wed 7 April
Pick-up: Paris Airport (CDG)   Drop-off: Paris Airport (CDG)
Avis - Economy 4 door
Manual transmission, Air Con   20.50 per day (including insurance)

£ 41.00 Price includes taxes and fees.

» ☐ I have read and accept the the rules and restrictions.

» ☐ I certify I meet all minimum driver requirements.

Now click CONFIRM to purchase tickets   [Confirm]

25. Check the two boxes at the bottom of the screen and click **Confirm** to complete the transaction.

26. Read the confirmation details and then click **Return** to go to the home page.

27. Go to a travel web site such as **www.expedia.co.uk** or **www.travelocity.com** and see how much it would cost to book your dream holiday.

28. The package should include flights, hotel, car hire and excursions if possible.

29. **Do not actually enter payment details unless you really want to take this holiday**. It is possible to go to the stage of getting prices before entering these details.

30. Obtain printouts showing the cost of the options you have chosen.

Education/Training Information

Most colleges and universities have their own web site, containing information for prospective and existing students. Course information is available and often you can enrol online. After starting a course, some establishments allow you to reserve library books over the Internet. Many have intranets, which hold useful information and course materials for enrolled students.

3

Exercise 78

1.   Go to the **Learners College** web site. You want to request information about a particular course.

2.   Select the **Contact** tab. Select **Course information** from the **Topic** drop down list.

3.   Enter your e-mail address and the following message.

4.   Click **continue**.

5.   When the next screen is displayed, click where indicated to return to the home page.

6.   Assume you have received an e-mail containing information about a course. To enrol, select the **Courses** button.

7.   Enter **digital photography** as the subject and select the **Part time** option.

8.   Click **go**. The list of available courses appears.

9.   There is only one suitable course. Click on the course title.

10. Read the information about the **Digital Photography** course.

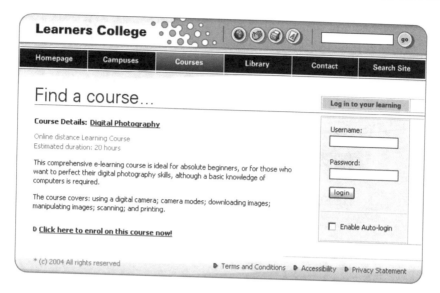

11. Click the link at the bottom of the page to enrol on the course.

12. Enter your details in the boxes provided and check the **rules and conditions** box. Click **continue**.

13. Enter **LcLogon** as your **Username** and **abc123** as the **Password**. Click **continue**.

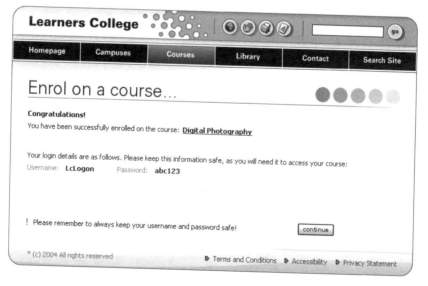

14. Click **continue** again and the home page is redisplayed. Now enrolled, you can research the subject before attending the first class by borrowing a library book. Select the **Library** button.

15. Enter **digital photography** in the **Subject/Book title** box and click **go**.

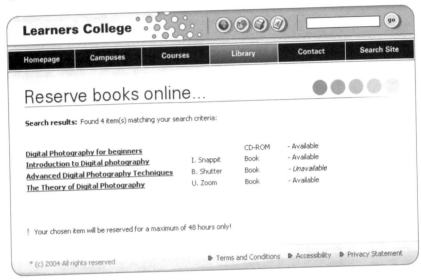

16. Select the book **Introduction to Digital photography** by clicking on the link.

17. Enter your **Username** as **LcLogon** and your **Password** as **abc123**.

18. Click **reserve it**.

19. When the confirmation message appears, click **continue**.

20. Find a web site for a college or university near to where you live.

21. Contact the college to request information about a course in a subject that you are interested in.

22. Find out if the web site contains the facility to reserve library books.

23. If it does, find out what the process is for doing this, e.g. do you have to register, how many items can you reserve?

Education/Training Participation

Some educational establishments, e.g. **learndirect** or the **Open University**, provide interactive learning environments. These are forms of distance learning, where you can complete a course online and are allocated a tutor for e-mail contact. It could be particularly useful for students who may be housebound, or have difficulty attending a course during normal opening hours.

Exercise 79

1. On the **Learners College** home page, click ⬚ **Log in to your learning** ⬚. The digital photography course you enrolled on in the previous exercise is a distance learning course.

2. Enter your **Username** as **LcLogon** and **abc123** as the **Password**. Click the **login** button to display a page with all your available courses.

3. You are only enrolled for one course. Click **Start my course** for the **Digital Photography** course. The course starts in a new window.

4. Select the learning topic **Module 2 - Camera modes**.

5. Work through the screens, reading the information on each one, but not making selections, then clicking **Next screen** until you reach screen 7 of 7.

6. Click the link to return to the module menu.

7. Select **Exit course** and then click **Logout** at the right of the screen.

8. Interactive courses require enrolment and often include a fee. This being the case, no specific instruction is given here. If you do wish to start a distance learning course, the **learndirect** or **Open University** web sites (**www.learndirect.co.uk** and **www.open.ac.uk**) may be a good place to start.

Employment

The Internet can help make it easier to look for employment. Many sites exist that allow you to look for a job, obtain information about it and even apply online, although interviews are still conducted face to face.

Exercise 80

1. Go to the home page of the **Learners Bank** web site. You have decided to enquire about job opportunities at the bank.

2. Click the ⊙ **Search for job opportunities** link.

3. As you have good people skills, select the **Customer Services** category and from the list of positions found, select **Tellers**. A job description is displayed.

4. The job sounds just the type of thing you were looking for. Click **Apply for this job online**.

5. Enter your name and address in the boxes provided and click **Next**.

6. Enter your e-mail address and date of birth and select the appropriate **Gender** option.

7. Click **Next**. Enter your qualifications in the box, pressing <**Enter**> after each one.

8. Click **Next** and list your work experience.

9. Click **Next** again and describe your general skills.

10. Click **Next** and on this screen describe any skills you have that make you ideal for the job.

11. Click **Next**.

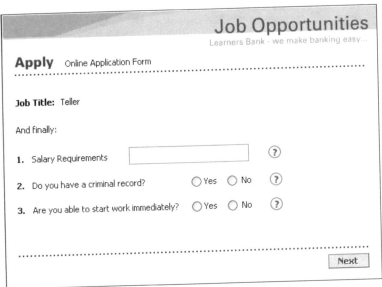

12. Complete the three questions and click **Next**.

13. If you have a copy of your CV on your computer, click **Browse** and locate it, if not, go to the next step.

> *An alternative to submitting a CV this way is to send it as an attachment to an e-mail message.*

14. Click **Submit**.

e-Citizen
© CiA Training Ltd 2004

Job Opportunities

Thank you...
Learners Bank - we make banking easy...

Your application has been received.

15. Click where indicated to return to the home page.

16. Go to **www.monster.co.uk** or **www.jobcentreplus.gov.uk**.

17. Notice if either site allows you to post (upload) your CV for potential employers to view.

18. Use the facilities to search for a job that interests you.

19. Display information about the job vacancy you have found.

20. If you are currently looking for employment, why not apply?

Health Information

Many health related web sites exist, but you should choose them with care to ensure the information you obtain from them is accurate and reliable. Well known health organisations such as **NHS Direct** and **Bupa** have informative web sites, but less formal information is available from many sources.

Exercise 81

1. Go to the **Learners Health** home page.

2. There is some information about the **Condition of the Week**. Click where indicated for more details.

3

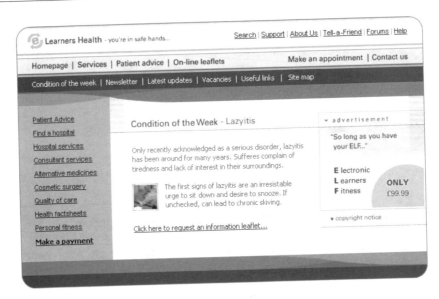

3. Read the symptoms of this worrying disease and then click the link beneath it to request an information leaflet.

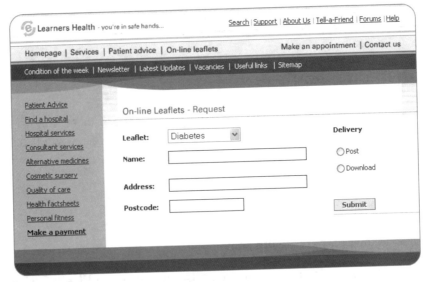

4. From the **Leaflet** drop down list, select **Lazyitis**, complete your name and address details and for the **Delivery** method, select **Post**.

5. Click **Submit** to send the request.

On-line Leaflets - Request

....

Request received...

Your leaflet will be sent to you within the next few days.
Thank you for your interest in Learners health services.

Click here to return to the homepage...

6.   Return to the homepage by clicking the link.

7.   Now go online and search for a site containing **health information**.

8.   Use the skills you have learned to get further information about a particular health issue that affects or concerns you. This can either be in the form of a leaflet, or by printing the information.

Health Appointments

It can be frustrating trying to telephone for an appointment with your doctor, as surgeries are usually very busy. It's not always convenient to book in person either. At the time of writing, the government is piloting a scheme where patients can arrange appointments online. Using the same technology used in booking flights or hotels, such a system could automatically check the availability of medical staff for a specified dates and/or times and offer a range of possible alternatives.

If this is successful, it will be expanded throughout the country.

Exercise 82

1.   Go to the home page of the **Learners Health** web site and click Make an appointment at the top of the screen.

3

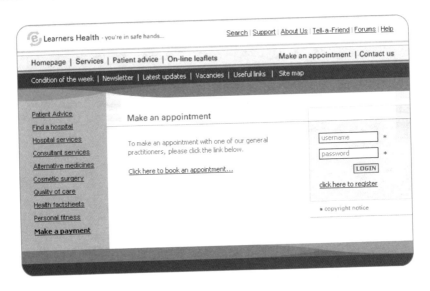

2.   Click the link to book an appointment.

3.   To avoid misuse, any process like this will be restricted to people who have previously registered with the system and obtained a user ID and password. You will have to log in now to continue. Enter the **Username** as **learner** and the **Password** as **health** and then click **Login**.

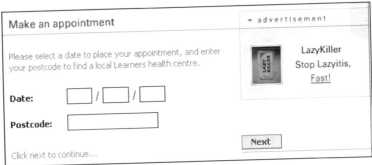

4.   Enter the date for which you want the appointment as **08/06** either this year or next, whichever is first.

5.   Enter the **Postcode** as **LV1 1AB** and click **Next**. The available appointments for the date required are displayed.

e-Citizen
© CiA Training Ltd 2004

6. Select the **10:30am** appointment with **Dr Chapman** and click **Next**.

7. At the confirmation screen, check the details and then click **Submit**.

8. Print the screen and then click where indicated to return to the home page.

Insurance

Many private health companies allow you to make claims online, as do insurance companies dealing with home and motor insurance. All such sites are restricted to people who are members with a policy number and usually a password provided by the company. The principles are pretty similar for each type of insurance and this exercise simulates making a claim for home insurance.

Exercise 83

1. Go to the **Learners Bank** web site and select the **Home Insurance** link at the left of the screen.

2. Click **Make a claim online now**.

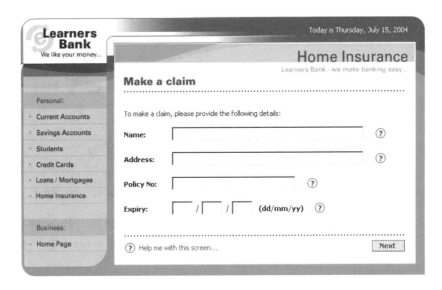

3. Enter your own name and address and the policy number **2468795**. The expiry date is one month from today. Enter this date now and click **Next**.

4. For **Type of loss** enter **Stolen dvd player**. Select the **Contents** option.

5. The **Location of loss** is **Lounge** and the date is today. Click **Next**.

6. Complete the following police incident details: **Police Case Number 2560**, **Police Department Learnersville Central**, **Loss Description Acme Luxury DVD Player**.

7. There is no criminal damage. Click **Submit**.

8. Click where indicated to return to the homepage.

9. Find out if the company providing your home insurance allows you to make online claims.

10. If you have a car, repeat the above step for your car insurer.

11. If you have health insurance, repeat step 9 for your health insurance company.

Interest Groups

Web sites often allow you to participate in discussion groups relating to many varied topics. Groups related to specific topics, such as surfing or knitting, are known as **special interest groups**. Search engines such as **Google** and **Yahoo** have their own dedicated discussion group areas. Some government (local or central) web sites allow you to participate in discussion groups relating to their policies, although this is usually to express views rather than dictate policy! It is normally required that you register before taking part in a discussion, but in the first steps below you don't need to do this. Other peoples' comments on a subject can be viewed and to take part, you can either comment on the same topic, or start a new discussion. These conversations are known as **threads**.

Exercise 84

1. Go to the **Learners Council** web site.

2. You are going to take part in a local government policy discussion group. Select the
   • Take part in our online discussion groups link.

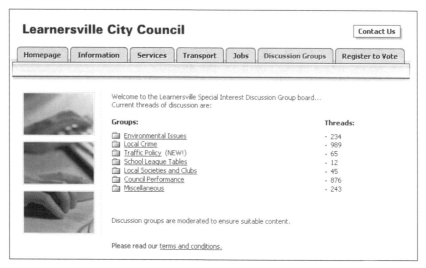

3. Select the **Traffic Policy** link to see this discussion thread.

4. Read the information about the traffic policy.

5. To see the most recent comment, click on the **I think more people should walk...** entry. Bill Tippings' comments are displayed.

6. Select the **Next >** link to see a further comment (from Ravi Singh).

7. Now select **< Back** to return to the main page for this thread.

8. You decide to make a comment on the subject. Click Post a reply to this thread.

9. Enter your e-mail address in the box provided and type a brief message stating your opinion about the bus lanes.

10. Click **Submit**. Notice that a link to your comment now appears at the top of the list as the most recent comment for this thread.

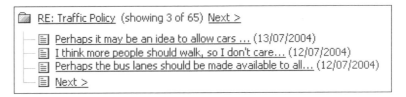

11. Select the **Homepage** tab.

12. Go to your local council web site and see if you can find any provision for discussion of council policy.

13. If so, post your views about a current policy. You may need to register to do this.

Business Information

As we have seen in **Block 2**, many organisations provide business information about their operations on web pages. As this could potentially take up a lot of space, sometimes the actual content is not shown and the user must submit a request to have the relevant information sent. The information can be sent in the post as hard copy, or sent to them as an e-mail attachment.

Many organisations now maintain an intranet of some kind to aid interchange of information amongst employees. This involves a number of networked PCs with the ability to share and transmit information between them. Some intranets will just act as notice boards to display consistent company information (such as Health and Safety notices, internal telephone lists) to all users, whilst others will allow more functionality with the ability to submit forms and connect to other applications.

Exercise 85

1. Open the **Learners Bank** web site and click on **Home Page** under **Business** in the **Navigation Pane**.

2. The bank's financial reports are not displayed here, but can be requested. Click the link to **Request this year's annual report**.

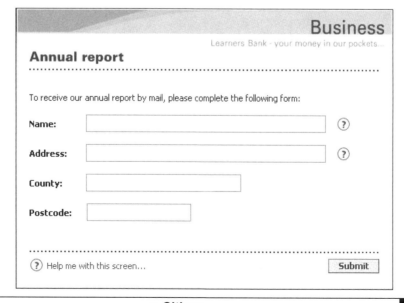

3. Fill in the request form with your own details and click **Submit**. A confirmation of receipt will be displayed. Click on the link to return to the **Learners Bank** home page.

4. Use the **Favorites** menu to return to the **Learners World** portal site. To see a simulated intranet site, click the **Added Extras** drop down arrow and select **Learners Intranet** from the list.

5. Like many intranets, you are required to logon to the system with a name and password. This identifies you to the system for any subsequent transactions. Enter a username of **Learner** and a password of **Training**.

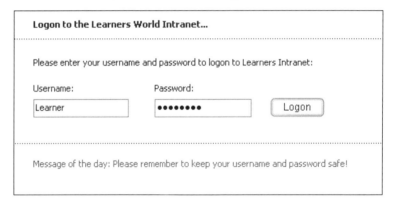

6. Click **Logon** to access the intranet system.

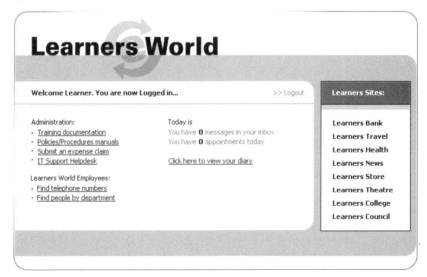

7. Some examples of typical intranet options are shown, such as displaying company information and contacting service departments. Notice that there is a link built into this system which would give you access to your data on an e-mail/organiser application, e.g. *Outlook* (**Click here to view your diary**). Click the **Submit an expense claim** link.

8. You are already logged into the system, so your name and details are added to the form automatically. Add some expense details and click **Total**.

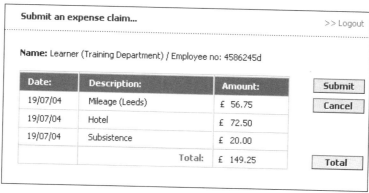

This is a sample form. A real form would contain more lines and require more data, such as codes to book the expenses against, VAT where relevant, etc.

9. If the details are correct, click **Submit** to send the form (the destination to which the information is sent is included in the design of the form).

10. When the confirmation screen is displayed, click the link to return to the main screen, then click **Logout**.

11. It will often be possible to create items yourself and post them to an intranet. Open *Word* and create a new document with the following content.

12. Select **File | Save as Web Page** to display the **Save As** dialog box. In a real situation you will need to know the exact location to save the web page. This would be supplied by your IT Administrator. For this exercise select the save location as the **Information** folder, leave the name as **July Sales Report** and click **Save**.

13. Close *Word*. Your report would now be available to any other intranet user who knew its location. Use the **Folders** view of **My Computer** to display the contents of **My Documents** and then the **Information** folder. Double click on **July Sales Report** to display it in the browser.

14. Close the **July Sales Report** browser window and the **My Computer** window.

15. Visit the site of a large commercial company. Use any of the examples in Exercise 65 if required.

16. Try and find a page which offers the option to request a copy of financial results.

17. Take a screen print of the page and include it in your **Pages Visited** folder.

18. It is difficult to visit an actual intranet site unless you are in an organisation which provides one. If you have access to such a site, take a screen print of the home page of the site and include it in your **Sites Visited** folder. If not, use the home page of the Learners World intranet site.

Exercise 86 - Revision: Participation

1. When buying goods online, at what point is the transaction actually completed?
    a) When the item is selected
    b) When credit card details are entered
    c) When credit card details are confirmed
    d) When you exit the site

2. In the real world, what would be the main reason for <u>not</u> buying goods online from the Learners Store site?
    a) They don't have enough choice
    b) It is not a secure site
    c) Prices are too expensive
    d) They don't offer free gifts

e-Citizen
© CiA Training Ltd 2004

3. With reference to the picture below, list the 5 different links which will change the page.

4. On the page above, if you wanted to add another item before buying, which link would you click? *CLICK HERE TO CONTINUE SHOPPING*

5. On sites selling goods or services, there is often a block of text defining the legal considerations governing the sale. What is the usual name for this text?

   a) Rules and Regulations

   b) Fixtures and Fittings

   c) Contents and Index

   d) Terms and Conditions ✓

6. The **Contact Us** option on a page often leads to a form which can be completed and submitted. Name two other ways used to contact someone using the Internet.
   E-MAIL   MESSAGE BOARD
   SEARCH BOX   CHAT ROOM

3

Block 3 Revision

This exercise covers all the topics introduced throughout the whole of Block 3.

Exercise 87

1. Where are items placed when making multiple purchases from an online store?

    a) Memory Cache

    b) Shopping Basket ✓

    c) Shopping Bag

    d) Hand bag

2. With reference to the picture below, what 3 form elements can be seen?

    a) Radio Buttons, Text Boxes, Drop Down Fields ✓

    b) Radio Buttons, Check Boxes, Drop Down Fields

    c) Text Boxes, Check Boxes, Drop Down Fields

    d) Radio Buttons, Text Boxes, Check Boxes

3. In a discussion group, a series of comments on a common theme is known as:

    a) A string

    b) A thread

    c) A loop

    d) A path

4. Go to **www.ciasupport.co.uk** and click the word **here** to enter the site. Select the link to **Online Forms** from the left of the page and read the information that is displayed.

5. Click the link to the **Booking Form**. This represents a form that you might need to submit to reserve a particular book from a library or college. Maximise the window if necessary.

6. Complete the form using the following information: your account is **AB42Z**, you want to borrow the book **Training Ferrets** by **Billy Weasel**. You need the book for next **Friday** and would like **e-mail** notification of its availability.

7. Print the completed form and then submit it. A confirmation screen will be displayed. Close the window to return to the **Online Forms** page.

8. Open the **Order Form**. This is a generalised form to order items from a catalogue. Complete the Billing information with your own details.

9. Order the following items: **2 adjustable widgets**, Product No **254**, **3 titanium doobies**, Product No **137**, and **1 plastic duck**, Product No **199**. Pay by **Visa** card, number **0123456789987654**, expiry date **05/07**. Your shipping address is the same as your billing address.

10. Print the form, submit it, then close the window.

11. Go to the **Learners World** intranet site and enter the username and password provided in Exercise 85.

12. Enter an expense claim for **Entertaining Clients** with today's date and a value of £160. Take a copy of the claim part of the page and paste it into your **Pages Visited** document.

13. Save and close the document.

14. Submit the claim. What is the reference number allocated to the claim?

   ⓘ *Answers are listed in the **Answers Section** at the end of the guide.*

Having completed the three Blocks, you are now ready to take your place in the online world as a responsible e-Citizen and to freely enjoy the opportunities that it offers.

3

Answers

Exercise 11

Q 1	b
Q 2	d
Q 3	c
Q 4	a

Exercise 17

Q 1	b
Q 2	c
Q 3	d
Q 4	c
Q 5	b

Exercise 27

Q 1	b
Q 2	b
Q 3	a, c and d are false b and e are true
Q 4	c
Q 5	a and c are false b and d are true

Exercise 28

Q 1	d
Q 2	f
Q 3	g
Q 4	a
Q 5	c
Q 6	b
Q 7	e

Exercise 32

Q 1	a) Menu Bar
	b) Toolbar
	c) Address Bar
	d) View window
	e) Status Bar
	f) Title Bar
	g) Links Bar
	h) Scroll Bar
	i) Taskbar
Q 2	c
Q 3	c only
Q 4	a) Favorites
	b) Home
	c) Refresh
	d) Back

Exercise 33

Q 1	Both
Q 2	E-mail
Q 3	Both
Q 4	Normal
Q 5	E-mail
Q 6	Normal
Q 7	Both

Exercise 42

Q 1   a
Q 2   d
Q 3   b
Q 4   a
Q 5   c
Q 6   c
Q 7   c
Q 8   b

Exercise 43 - Block 1 Revision

Q 1   c
Q 2   a
Q 3   c
Q 4   c
Q 5   b
Q 6   d
Q 7   b
Q 8   d
Q 9   c
Q 10   d

Exercise 48

Q 1   c
Q 2   d
Q 3   b
Q 4   b
Q 5   b
Q 6   a

Exercise 49

Q 1   True
Q 2   False
Q 3   False
Q 4   True
Q 5   False
Q 6   True
Q 7   False
Q 8   True

Exercise 51

a)   Internet
b)   firewall
c)   filters
d)   software
e)   configured
f)   protection
g)   traffic

Exercise 53

Q 1   Encryption is the scrambling of information before it is transmitted over the Internet. The scrambling is based on a key supplied by the web site (a bank for example) and can only be unscrambled at the other end by means of a matching key in their possession.

Q 2   Encryption is used so that even if sensitive information is intercepted, it will only be readable with the relevant keys.

Exercise 53 - Continued

Q 3   Secure sites are recognised by **https** in the **URL** and a padlock symbol on the **Taskbar**.

Q 4   You should take care that your keystrokes are not observed as you are typing sensitive data such as passwords.

Exercise 54

Q 1   False

Q 2   True

Q 3   True

Q 4   False

Q 5   False

Exercise 55

Q 1   b

Q 2   d

Q 3   d

Q 4   b

Q 5   d

Q 6   c

Q 7   a

Q 8   d

Exercise 66

Q 1   a) Tabs

b) Navigation Pane

c) Link (or hyperlink)

Q2   Australia

Q3   2

Q4   Widgets

Q 5   a) Learners Health

b) Learners Council

c) Learners Bank

Q 6   a) A **Council** site

b) A **News** site

c) A **Store** site

Exercise 67 - Block 2 Revision

Q1   a

Q2   c

Q3   d

Q4   watergate -washington -nixon

Q 5 a) Joseph Cyril Bamford (jcb founder)

b) Lincoln City (nebraska capital)

c) James Earl Carter Jnr, 01/10/24 ("jimmy carter" president)

Q6   Kurt Hahn, Prince Philip

Q7   0.5% interest

Q8   The Singh family

Q11   22 Mildew Street

Q12   West of Green Park, 250 places

Exercise 69

Q1   Any four from the following: text box, drop down field, option button, check box, submit button, reset button.

Q2   The reset button will clear information from a form.

Q3   The statement is false.

Q4   A padlock indicates a secure server.

Exercise 86

Q1   c

Q2   b

Q3   Proceed to checkout, Continue shopping, and 3 links to remove an item and redisplay this page.

Q4   Click here to continue shopping.

Q5   d

Q6   E-mail, Discussion Groups, Chat Rooms.

Exercise 87 - Block 3 Revision

Q1   b

Q2   a

Q3   b

Q14   **CF5981Z**

Glossary

Address Bar
Shows the address of the page currently displayed in the browser and allows entry of a new address to be visited.

Application software
Software programs that allow a PC to perform specific tasks.

Attachment
Any file transmitted with an e-mail.

Bookmark
A named position in a document used by a hyperlink or to add an address to your favourites list.

Broadband
A high speed, always live, Internet connection.

Browser
The application that controls your interface with the World Wide Web.

Checkout
The page in a online shopping site where all the selected items can be reviewed and paid for.

Desktop
The initial computer screen, displaying icons and the **Taskbar** along the bottom of the screen.

Dial-up Connection
A method of connecting to the Internet that requires a modem on the computer dialling the number of a server.

Distance Learning
An educational course which can be followed remotely (either by post or internet) without attendance at a specific establishment.

Domain Name
The address of a computer that sends and receives mail.

Download
Transfers an object from a web site to the user's computer.

File
The name given to a named unit of information saved electronically.

File Management
The process of copying, moving, creating and deleting folders and files.

File Types	A three letter code at the end of every file name, which indicates what type of file it is and what application can be used to process it, e.g. **Letter.doc** is a *Word* document.
Floppy Disk Drive	In principle, the same as an hard disk drive though storage capacity is far smaller. Holds information on a 3.5 inch floppy disk.
Folder	A method of grouping together files (and other folders).
Font	A type or style of print.
Format	The process of preparing a storage disk for use.
Formatting	Changing the visual appearance of data.
Forward (a message)	Send a copy of an e-mail which you have received, to another address, with an optional message of your own.
Hard Disk Drive	A form of data storage capable of holding vast amounts of information, commonly called an HDD.
Hardware	Any physical part of a computer system.
History	A list of web pages visited recently.
Home Page (1)	The main page in a site, with links to all other pages.
Home Page (2)	Your Home Page is the page displayed when the Browser starts and when you click the **Home** button.
Hyperlink	Area of a page which can be clicked to move to a different location, usually a different web page.
Inbox	The default folder for storing all incoming e-mail messages.
Input device	Any device that allows a user to enter data into a computer.
Internet	A global network of linked computers.
Intranet	An organisation's internal network.

ISP	Internet Service Provider - Companies which provide Internet access.
Keyboard	An input device used to enter information into a computer.
Link	Abbreviation for **Hyperlink**.
Login	A process of establishing your identity as a person entitled to access a specific website.
Maximize	Increase the window to fill the screen.
Minimize	Reduce an application to an icon on the **Taskbar**.
Modem	Standing for Modulator - Demodulator, this is a device that converts information allowing it to pass from computer to computer via a telephone line.
Monitor	A visual display device connected to a computer.
Mouse	An input device used primarily for navigation around a computer's desktop.
Multimedia	An application or function that involves many techniques such as text, sound and video.
Navigation	Moving around between web sites or the pages within a site.
Offline	Without having a current connection to the Internet.
Online	Having a current connection to the Internet.
Operating System	The piece of software which runs "behind" all others, the operating system allows all other software to run. Examples are *Microsoft Windows* and *Unix*.
Outbox	The folder for storing outgoing e-mails before they have been sent.
Output device	Any device that allows a user to bring stored data out of a computer.
PC	Personal Computer.

Peripheral	A device attached to a computer, e.g. printer.
Preview Pane	An area of the **Inbox** display screen where the contents of messages can be viewed without opening them.
Print Preview	A pictorial view of how something will print.
Recycle Bin	An area of storage where deleted files are held temporarily before being deleted completely.
Refresh	Redisplays the most recent version of the current page.
Scroll Bars	A system of viewing hidden information when the whole window is not displayed.
Search Engine	A web site which allows the searching of the web for information.
Sent Items	The folder for storing outgoing e-mails after they have been sent.
Server	A single computer on a network from which other machines derive resources.
Software	The programs that run on a computer.
Speakers	Output devices which play sounds.
Taskbar	A bar across the bottom of window, showing current application icons.
Virus	A malicious piece of code which can cause damage to computerised systems.
Web Page	A storage facility for Internet information
Word	*Microsoft Word*. A word processing application.
World-Wide-Web	The collection of information stored on the Internet.

Index

Useful Web Sites

There is no guarantee that these sites will always be available, as web sites come and go. Here are few to try, enjoy your surfing.

Auctions
www.ebay.co.uk   buy or bid, everything is here

Books and CDs
www.amazon.co.uk   find that book or CD
www.studentbookworld.com   for academic books

Chat
www.aol.co.uk   download AOL instant messenger

Computers
www.pcworld.co.uk   the computer superstore

Education
www.bbc.co.uk/education   learning for all ages
www.learndirect.co.uk   adult learning courses

Financial
www.ft.com   Financial Times
www.thisismoney.com   money news and advice

Government
www.open.gov.uk   entry point for Government info

Health
www.bupa.co.uk   private health
www.nhsdirect.nhs.uk   health advice

Hobbies and Pastimes
www.antiques.co.uk   find and buy antiques online
www.betterphoto.com   learn to take better pictures
www.crocus.co.uk   buy plants online
www.diy.com   B&Q the DIY superstore
www.friendsreunited.co.uk   catch up with your school friends
www.greatbuildings.com   buildings, 3D models, photos etc
www.nationaltrust.org.uk   visit historically interesting places
www.rfu.com   rugby union
www.ski.co.uk   a ski directory
www.whatsonstage.com   home of the British theatre

Humour

www.funny.co.uk	have a laugh
www.funnytimes.com	funny cartoons

Kids

www.bbc.co.uk/cbbc	children's BBC
www.disney.com	where the magic lives on
www.mamamedia.com	the place for kids on the net
www.teen.com	the ultimate place for teenagers
www.yucky.com	for science and biology

Jobs

www.careerguide.net	a career advice resource
www.gisajob.co.uk	search for your next job here

Motoring

www.dvla.gov.uk	the Driving & Vehicle Licensing Agency
www.driving.co.uk	driving issues and tuition
www.rac.co.uk	the RAC, includes route planning
www.whatcar.co.uk	buying, news, road tests, etc.

Museums

www.louvre.fr	France's treasure house
www.thebritishmuseum.ac.uk	browse the collection
www.guggenheim.org	the Guggenheim museum
www.uffizi.firenze.it/welcome.html	the Uffizi Gallery in Florence

News

www.bbc.co.uk/news	keep up with the news
www.cnn.com	American based news
www.sky.com/news	the ultimate news site

Property

www.propertyfinder.co.uk	find a new house

Puzzles

www.thinks.com	quizzes, puzzles, word searches

Search Engines
www.ask.co.uk   ask Jeeves, type in a question
www.google.co.uk   easy to use

Shopping
www.kelkoo.co.uk   compare prices before you buy
www.tesco.co.uk   superstore

Tax
www.inlandrevenue.gov.uk   tax information

Telecommunications
www.bt.com   telephone services
www.yell.co.uk   let your fingers do the walking

Travel
www.expedia.co.uk   book a holiday
www.ferrybooker.com   book a ferry crossing
www.easyjet.com   book a flight
www.thetrainline.co.uk   buy a train ticket

Weather
www.met-office.gov.uk   get the weather forecast

Record of Achievement Matrix

This Matrix is to be used to measure your progress while working through the guide. This is a learning reinforcement process, you judge when you are competent.

Tick boxes are provided for each feature. 1 is for no knowledge, 2 is for some knowledge and 3 is for competent. A section is only complete when column 3 is completed for all parts of the section.

For details on sitting e-Citizen Examinations in your country please contact the local ECDL Licensee, or visit the European Computer Driving Licence Foundation Limited web site at http://www.ecdl.com.

Tick the Relevant Boxes **1**: No Knowledge **2**: Some Knowledge **3**: Competent

Block 1	No	Exercise	1	2	3
1 The Computer	1	Introduction to the Computer			
	2	Starting the Computer			
	3	The Windows Desktop			
	4	The Mouse			
	5	The Start Menu			
	6	Windows			
	7	Manipulating Windows			
	8	Scroll Bars			
	9	Dialog Boxes			
	10	Shut Down and Restart the Computer			
2 Simple Applications	12	Running an Application			
	13	Entering and Formatting Text			
	14	Saving Work			
	15	Printing Documents			
	16	Closing an Application			
3 Files and Folders	18	File Storage			
	19	Folders and Files			
	20	Folders View			
	21	File Types			
	22	Creating New Folders			
	23	Copying Files and Folders			
	24	Moving Files and Folders			
	25	Deleting Files and Folders			
	26	Using Help			

e-Citizen

8 Information

	56	Introduction to Learners World			
	57	News			
	58	Government			
	59	Consumer			
	60	Travel			
	61	Education/Training			
	62	Employment			
	63	Health			
	64	Interest Groups			
	65	Business			

Block 3

9 Online Services

	68	Online Forms			
	69	Online Security			

10 Participation

	70	News			
	71	Government Services			
	72	Government Submitting Information			
	73	Consumer Banking			
	74	Consumer Shopping			
	75	Consumer Booking Tickets			
	76	Consumer Paying Bills			
	77	Travel			
	78	Education/Training Information			
	79	Education/Training Participation			
	80	Employment			
	81	Health Information			
	82	Health Appointments			
	83	Insurance			
	84	Interest Groups			
	85	Business Information			

Other Products from CiA Training

If you have enjoyed using this guide you can obtain other products from our range of over 150 titles. CiA Training Ltd is a leader in developing self-teach training materials and courseware.

Open Learning Guides

Teach yourself by working through them in your own time. Our range includes products for: Windows, Word, Excel, Access, PowerPoint, Project, Publisher, Internet Explorer, FrontPage and many more... We also have a large back catalogue of products; please call for details.

European/International Computer Driving Licence

We produce accredited training materials for the European Computer Driving Licence (ECDL/ICDL) qualification. Material produced covers a variety of Microsoft Office products from Office 97 to 2003.

Advanced European/International Computer Driving Licence

We produce accredited training materials for the Advanced European Computer Driving Licence (ECDL/ICDL) qualification. The four main products cover Word Processing, Spreadsheets, Databases and Presentations. Material produced covers a variety of Microsoft Office products from Office 97 to 2003.

Trainer's Packs

Specifically written for use with tutor led I.T. courses. The trainer is supplied with a trainer guide (step by step exercises), course notes (for delegates), consolidation exercises (for use as reinforcement) and course documents (course contents, pre-course questionnaires, evaluation forms, certificate template, etc). All supplied on CD with the rights to edit and copy the documents.

Purchasing Options

The above publications are available in a variety of purchasing options; as single copies, class sets and or site licences. However, Trainer's Packs are only available as site licences.

Conventional Tutor Led Training

CiA have been successfully delivering classroom based I.T. training throughout the UK since 1985. New products are constantly being developed; please call to be included on our mailing list. Information about all these materials can be viewed at *www.ciatraining.co.uk*.